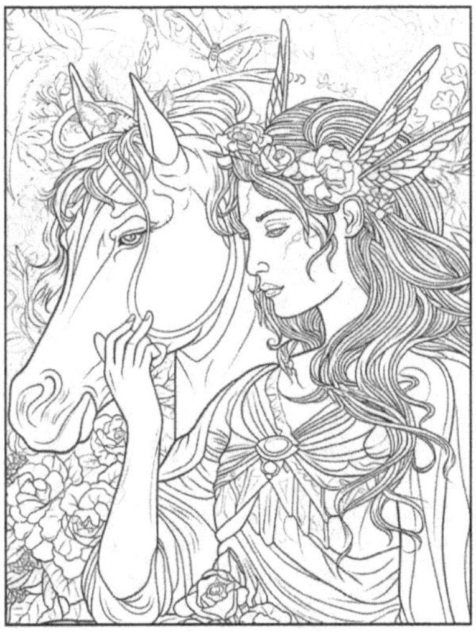

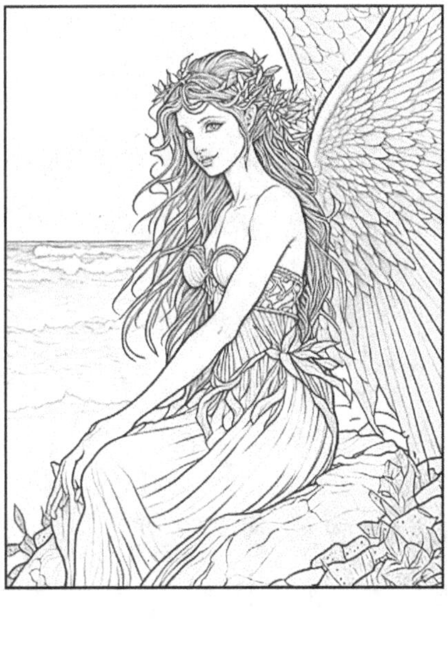

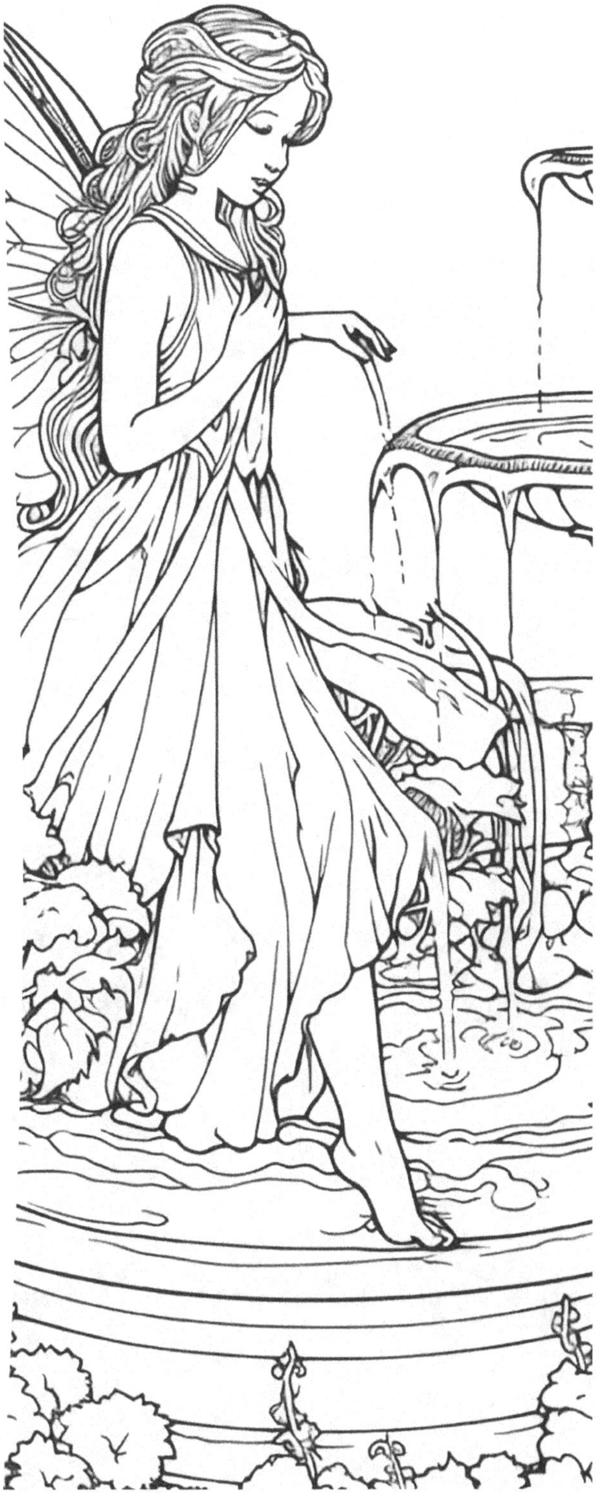

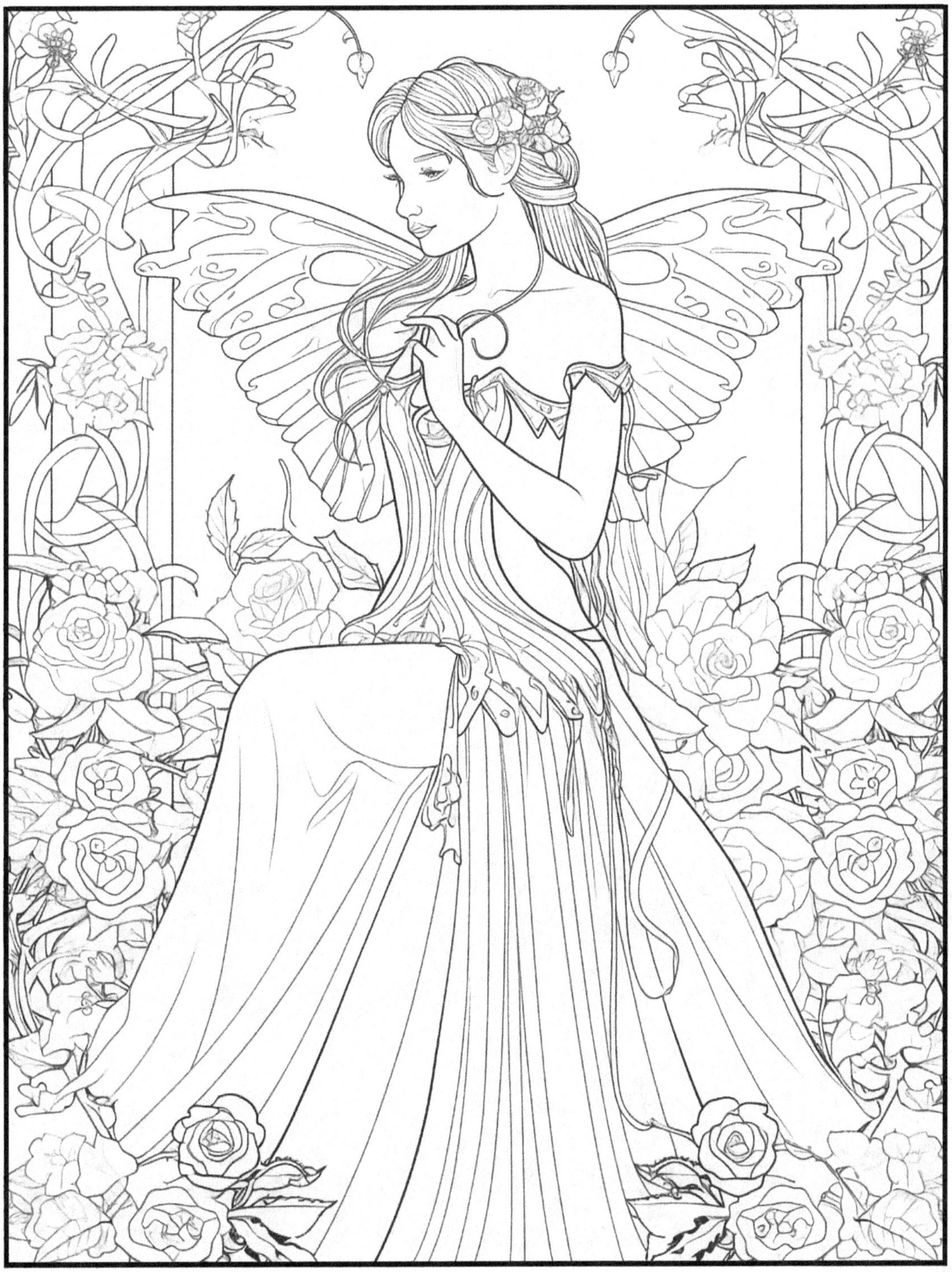

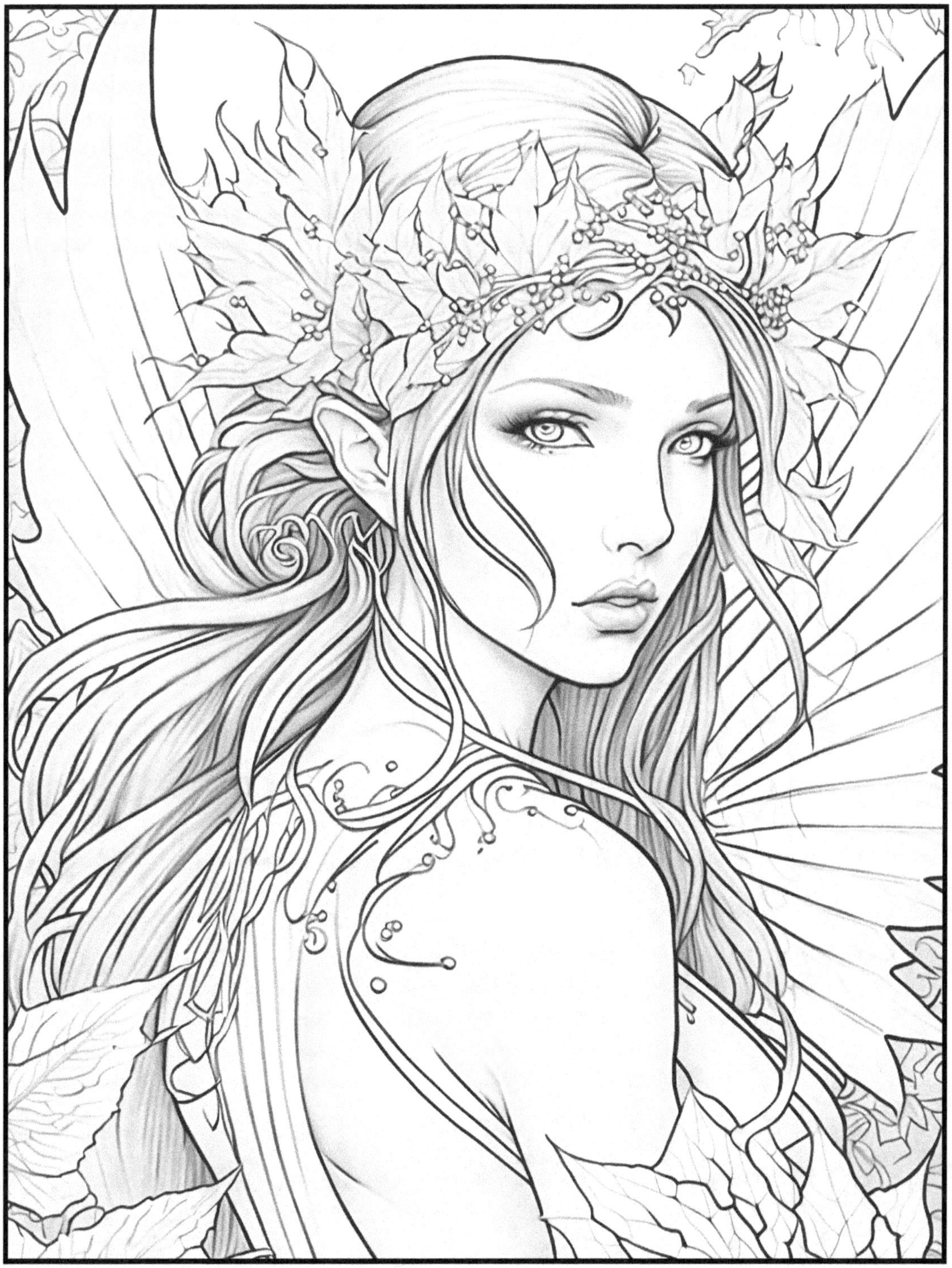

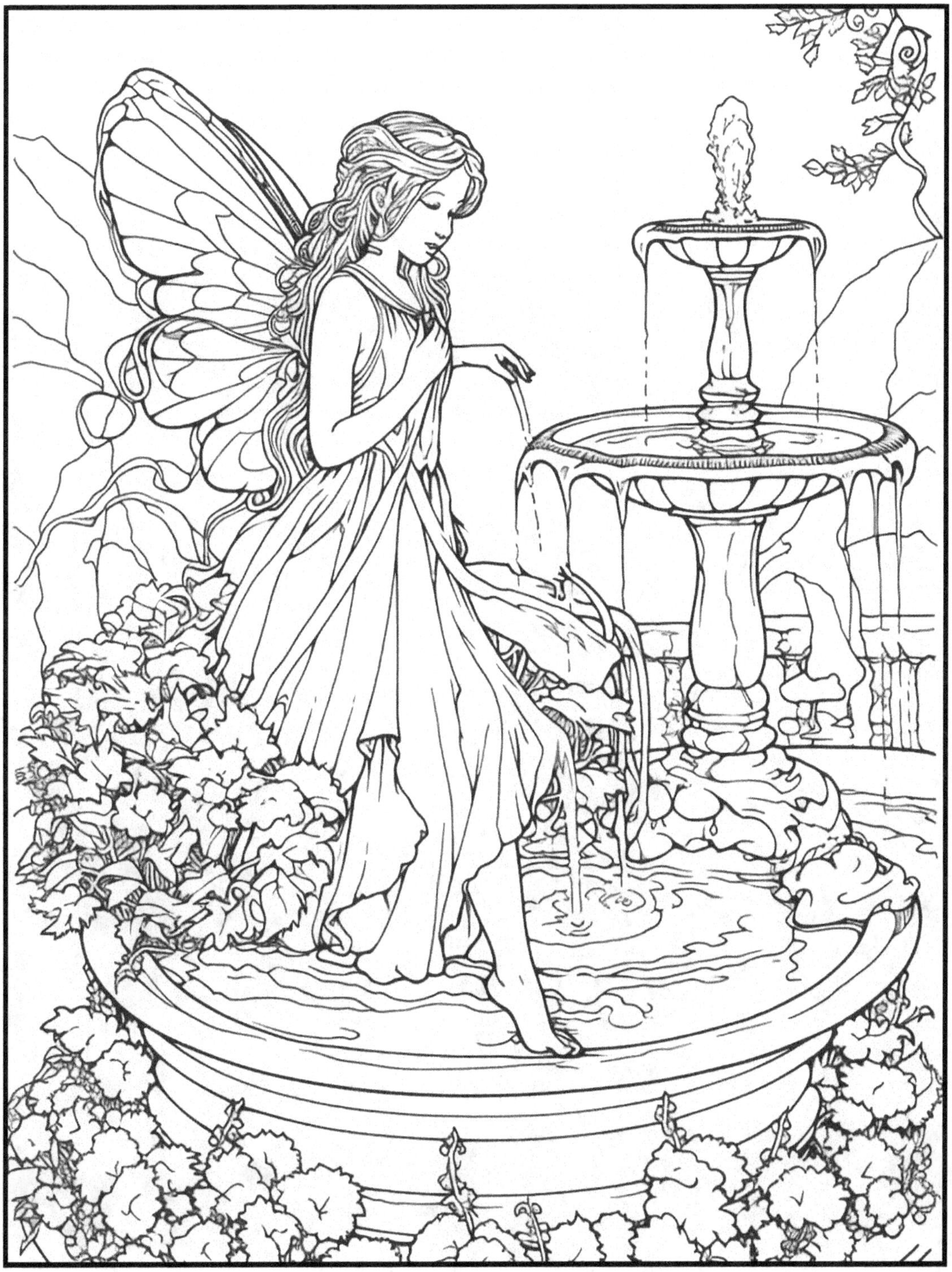

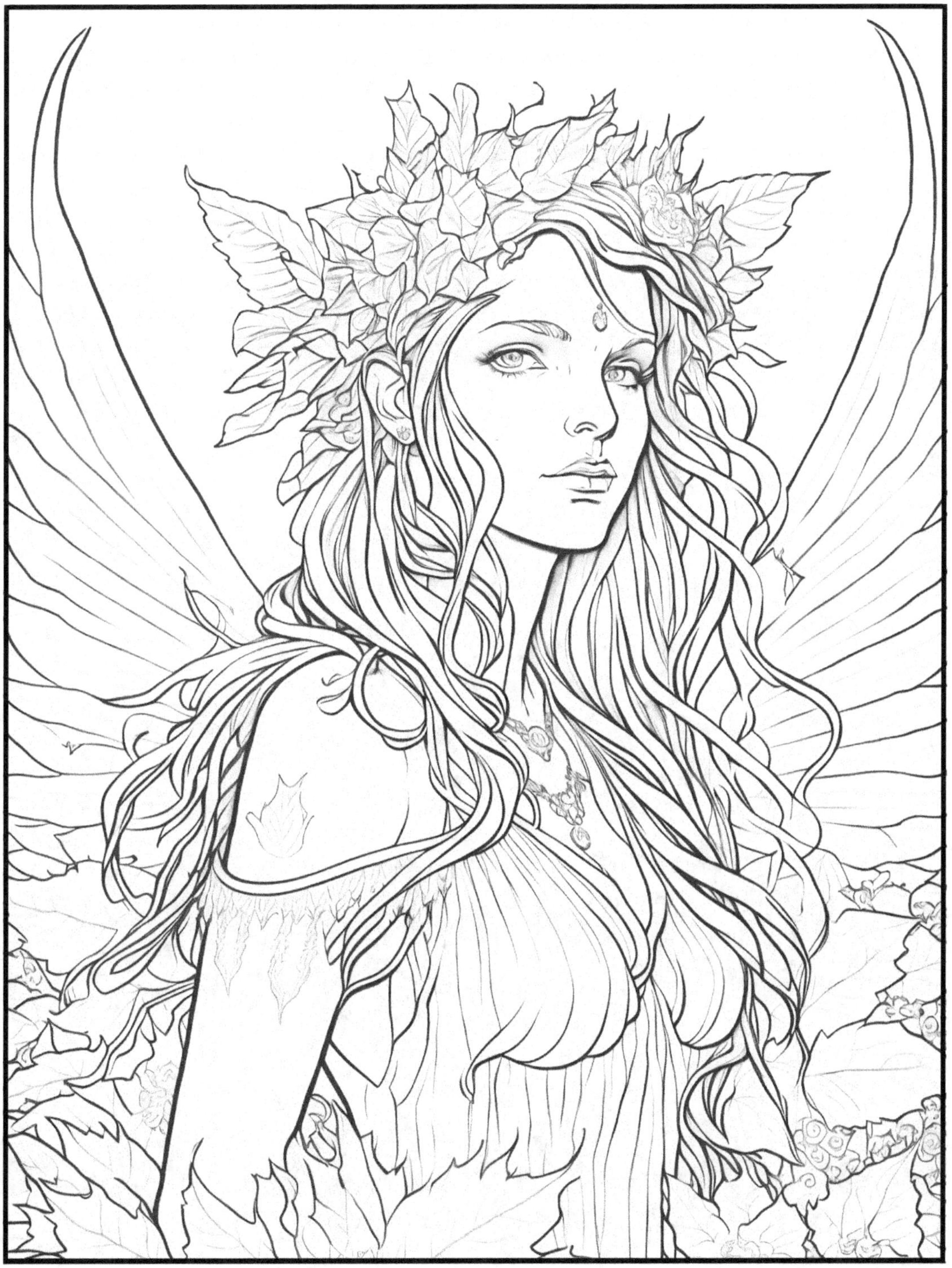

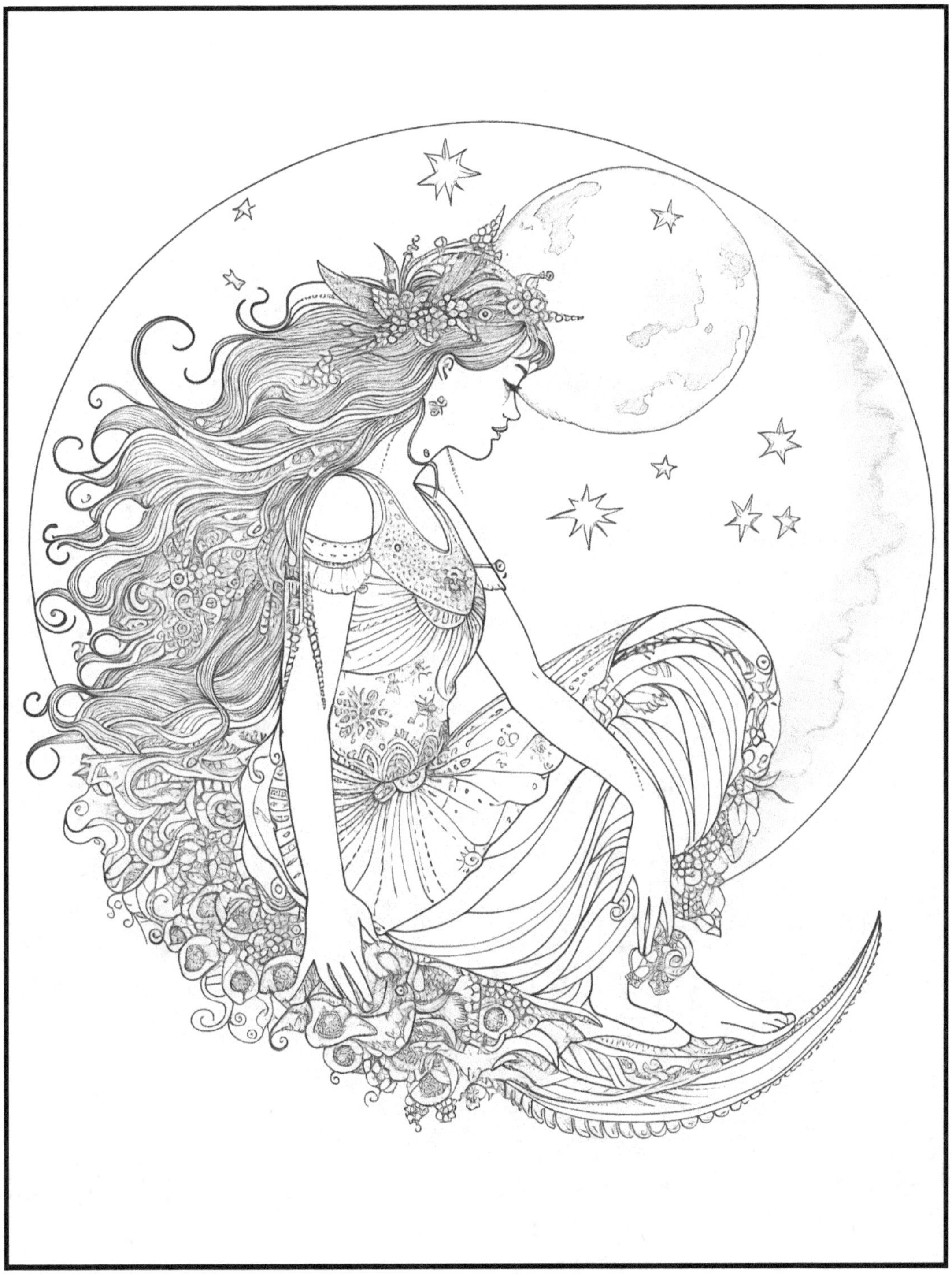

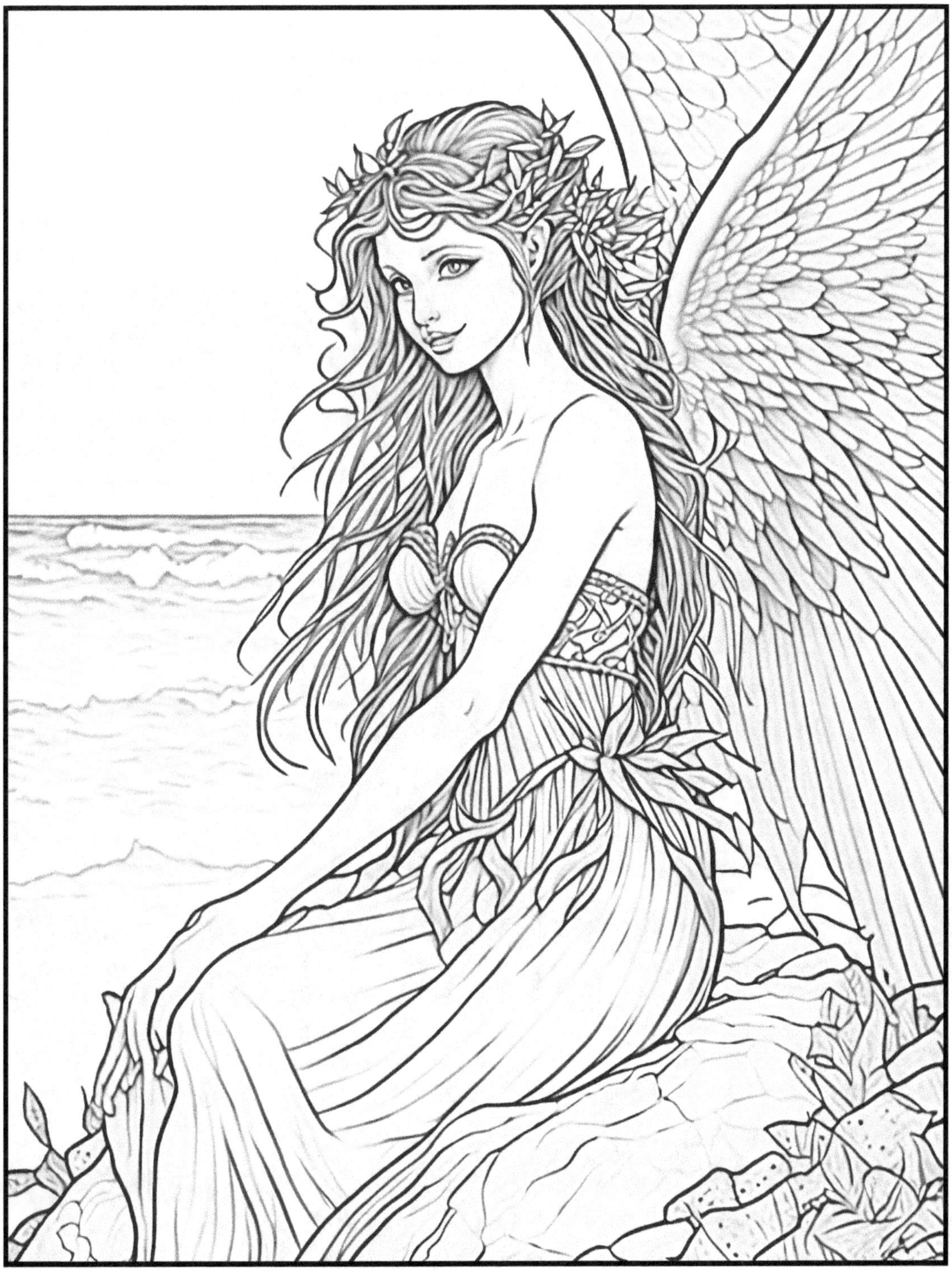

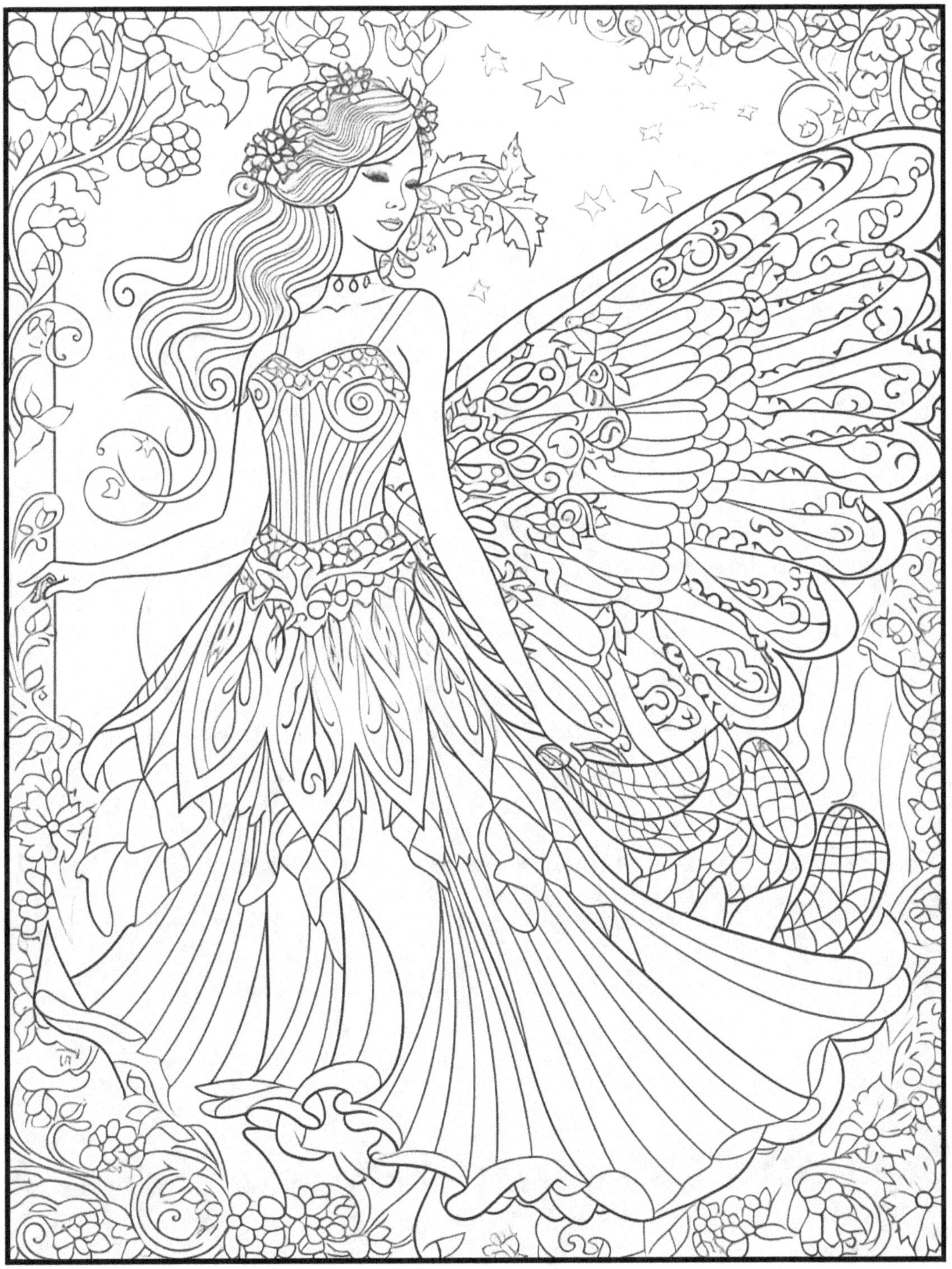

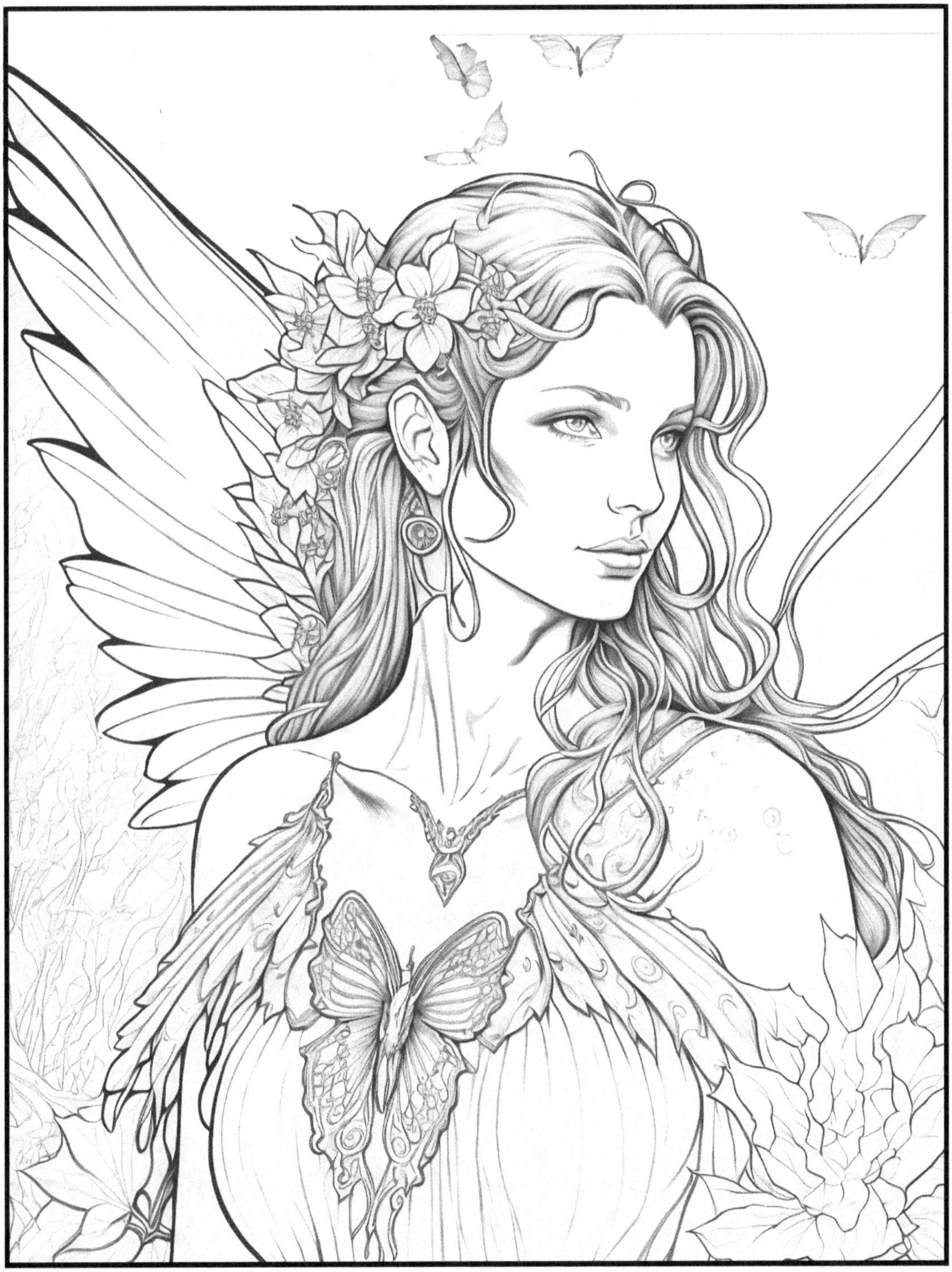

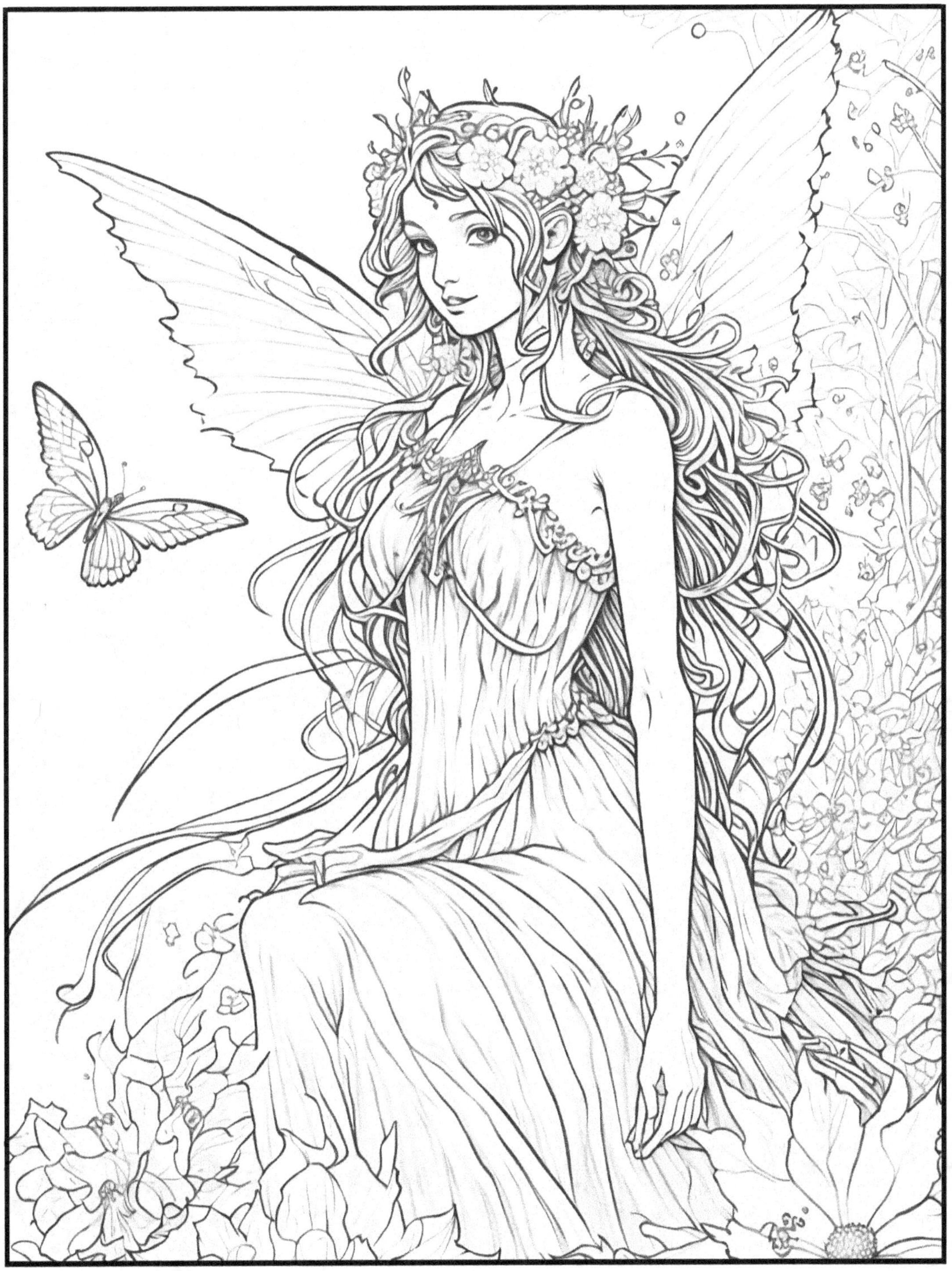

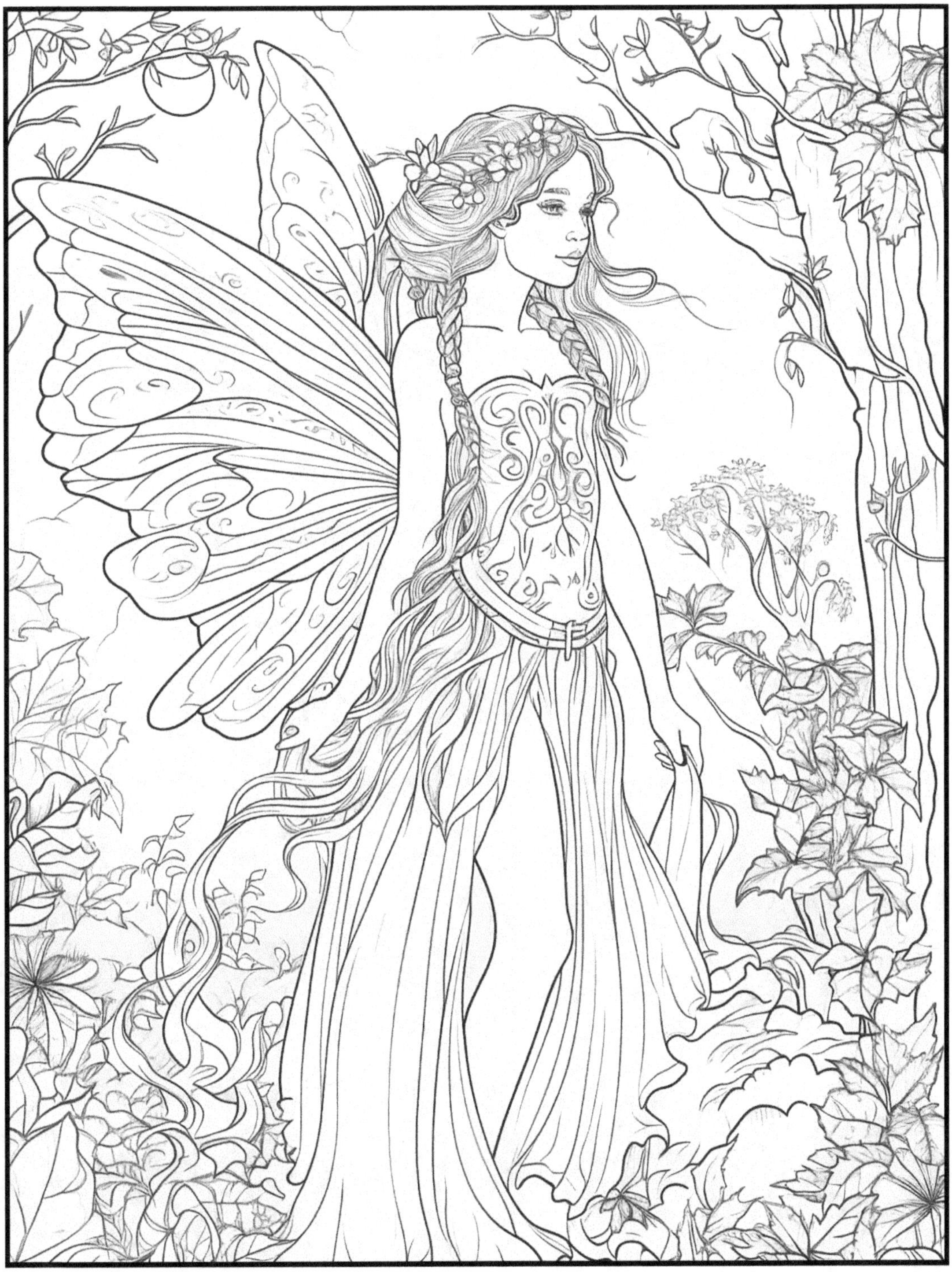

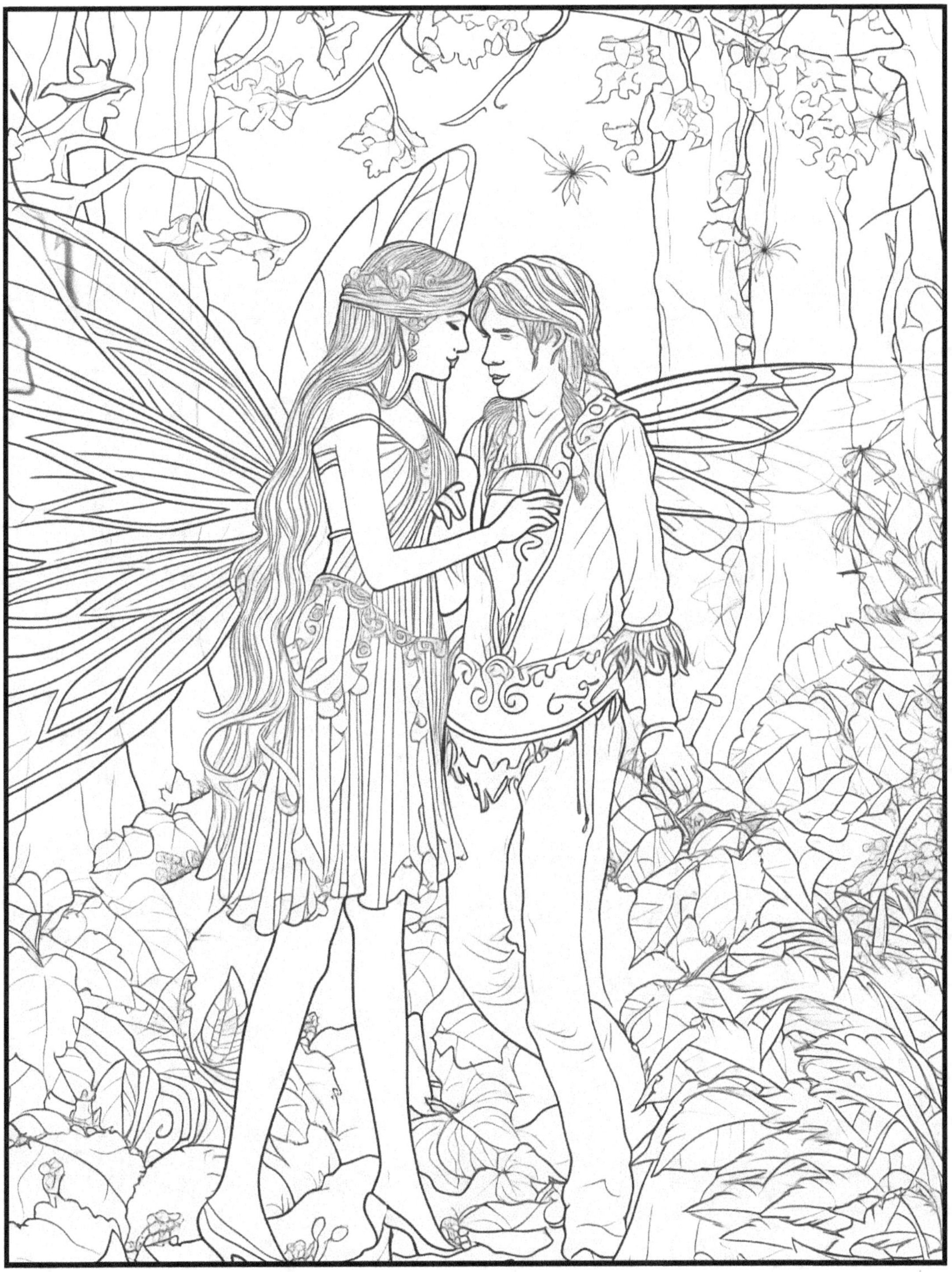

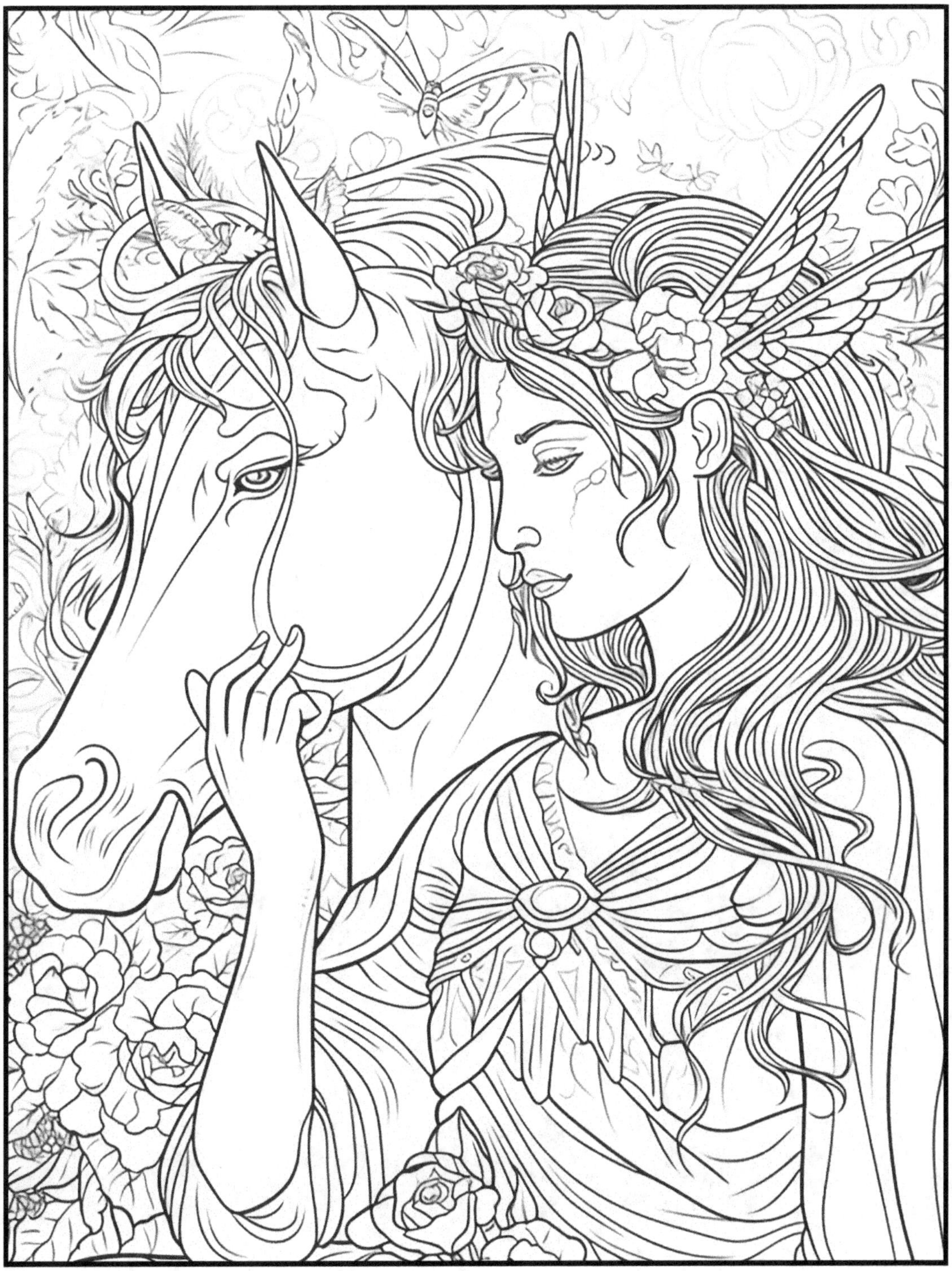

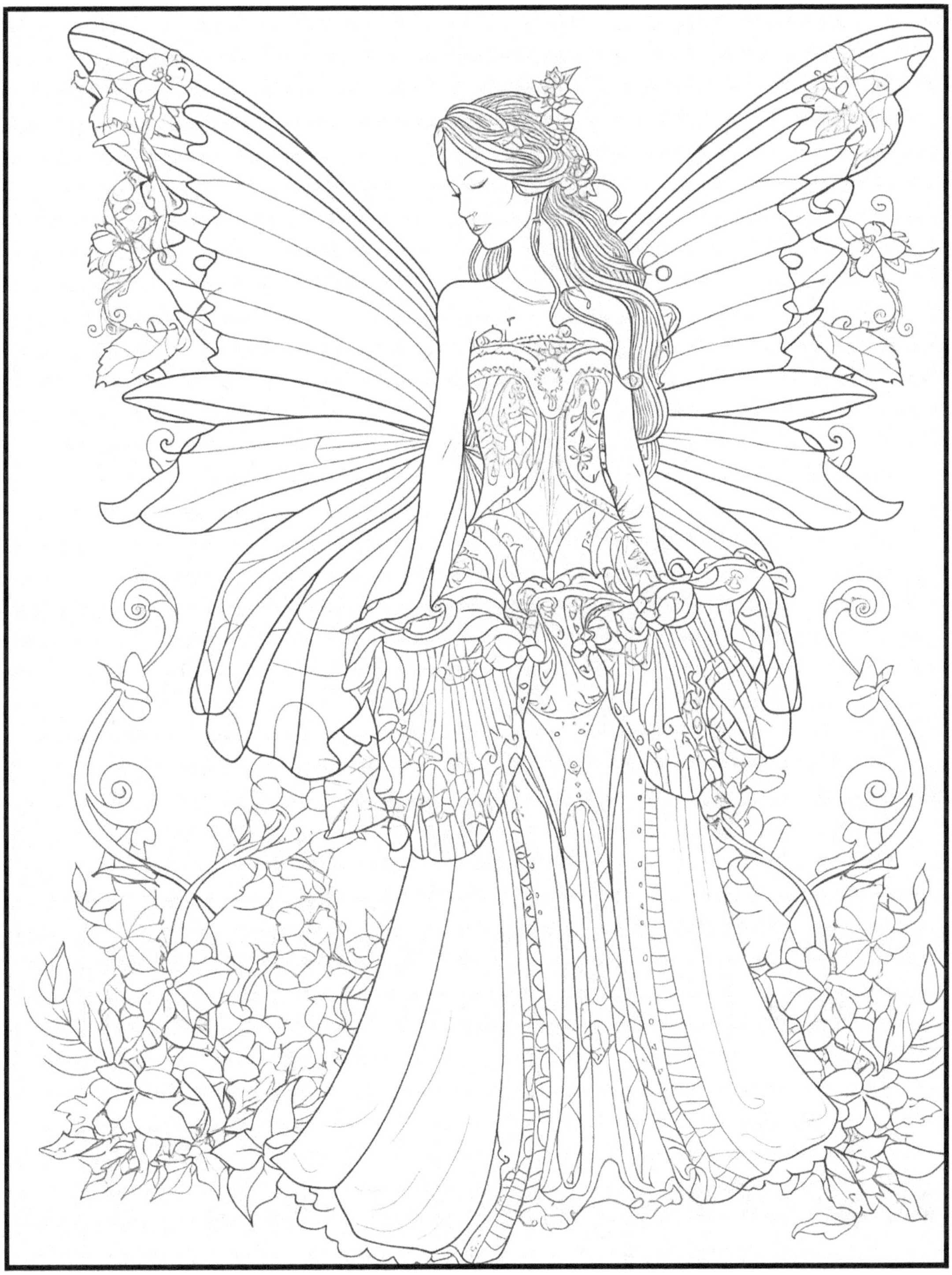

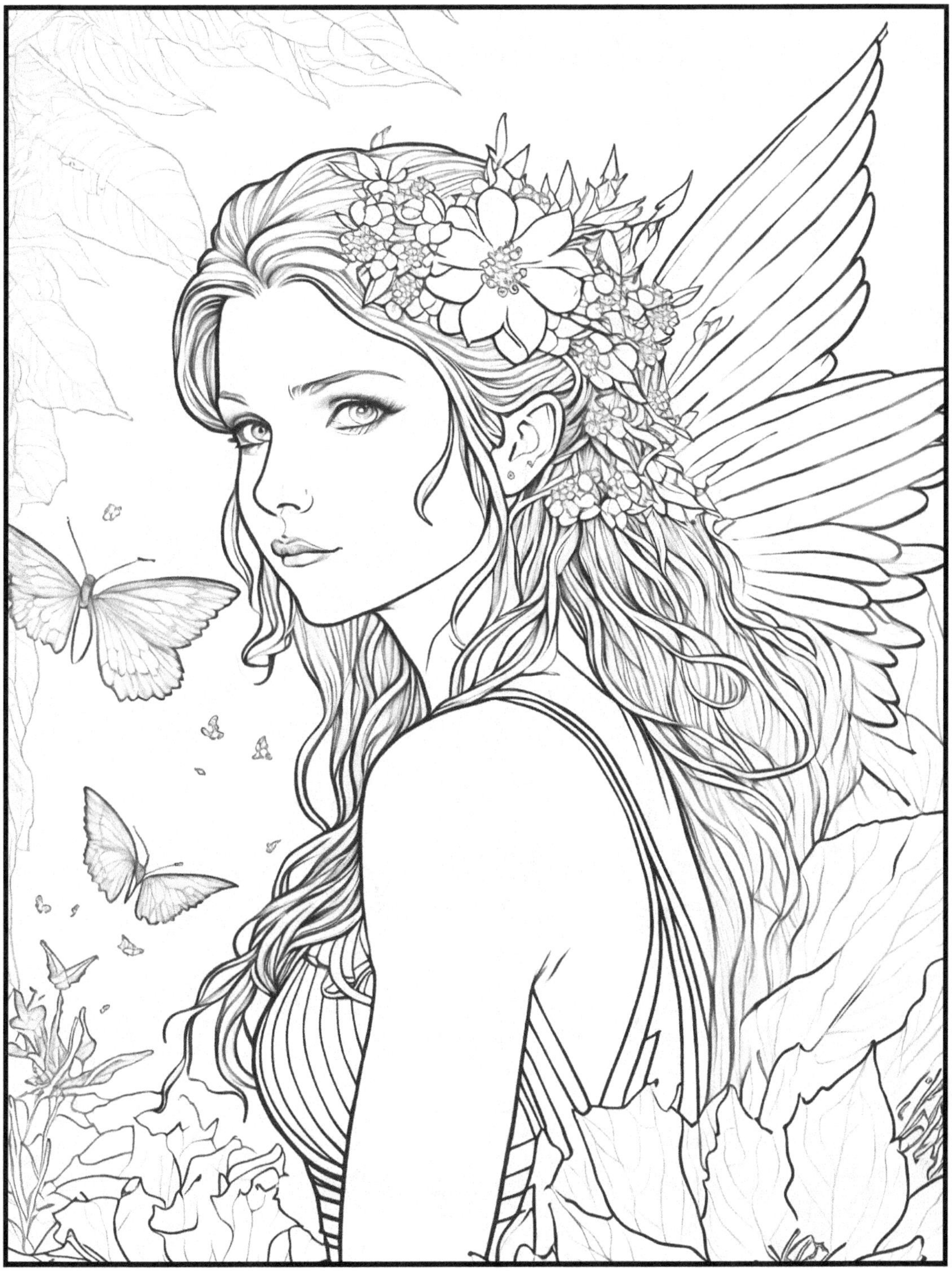

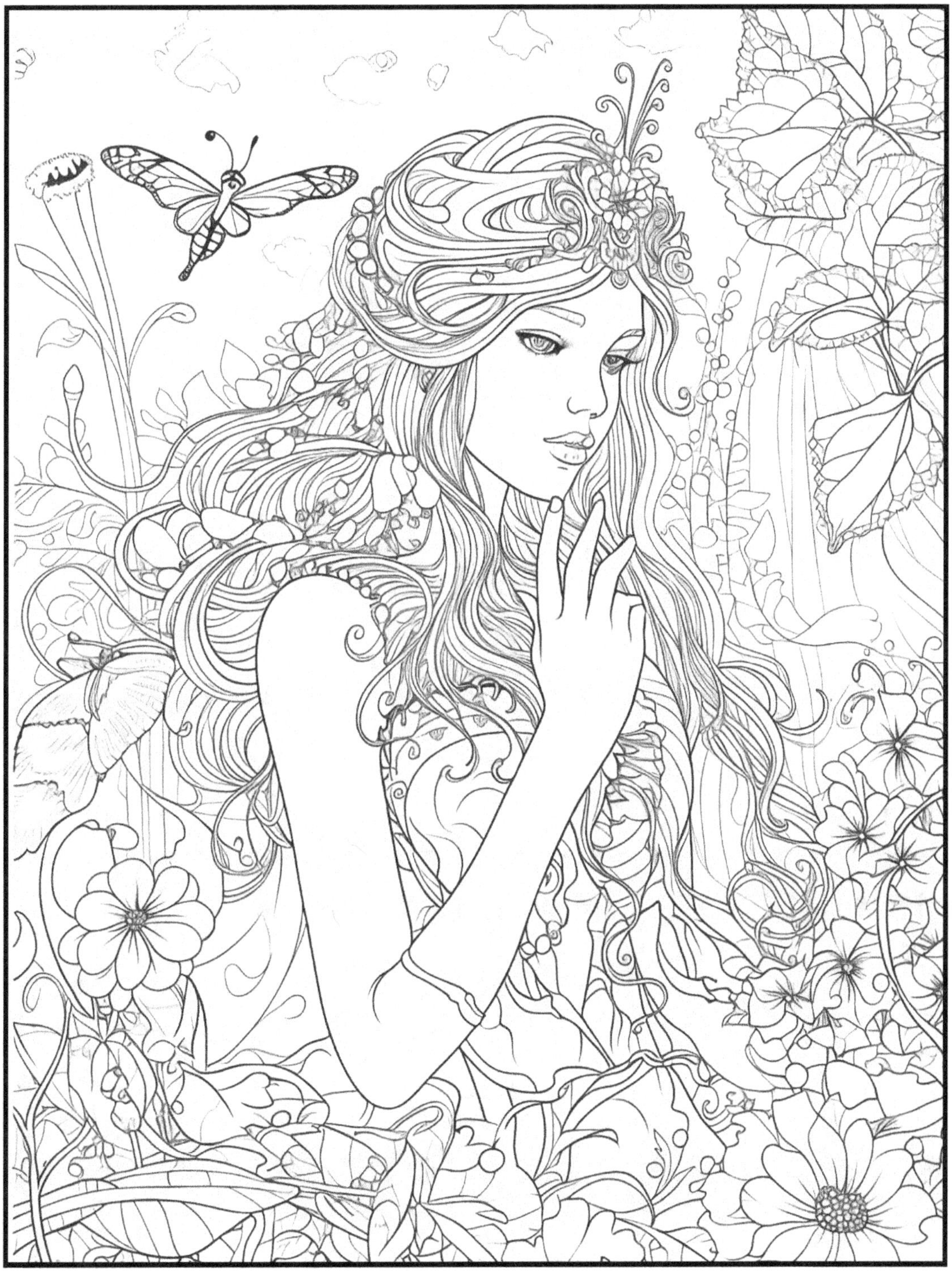

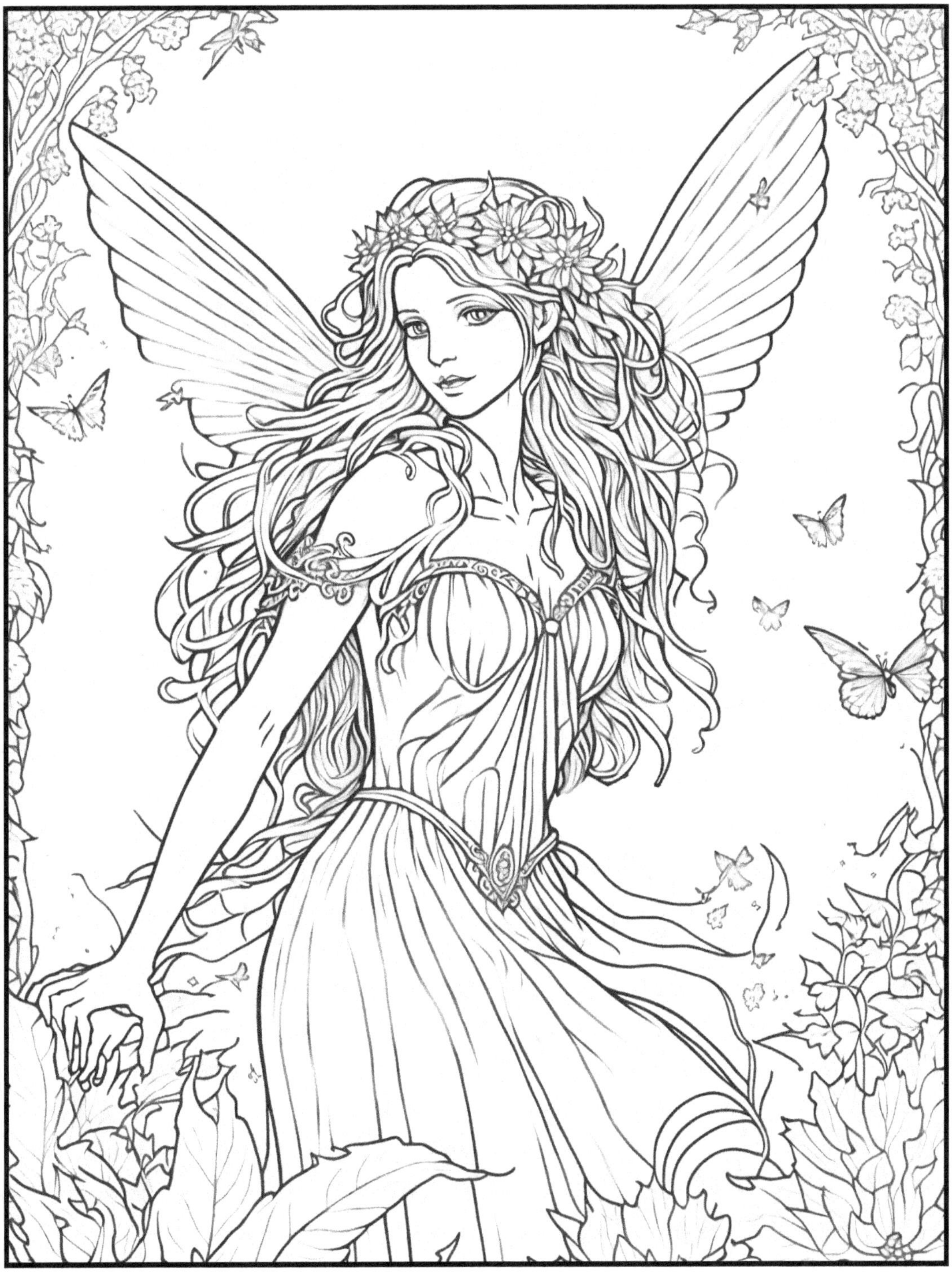

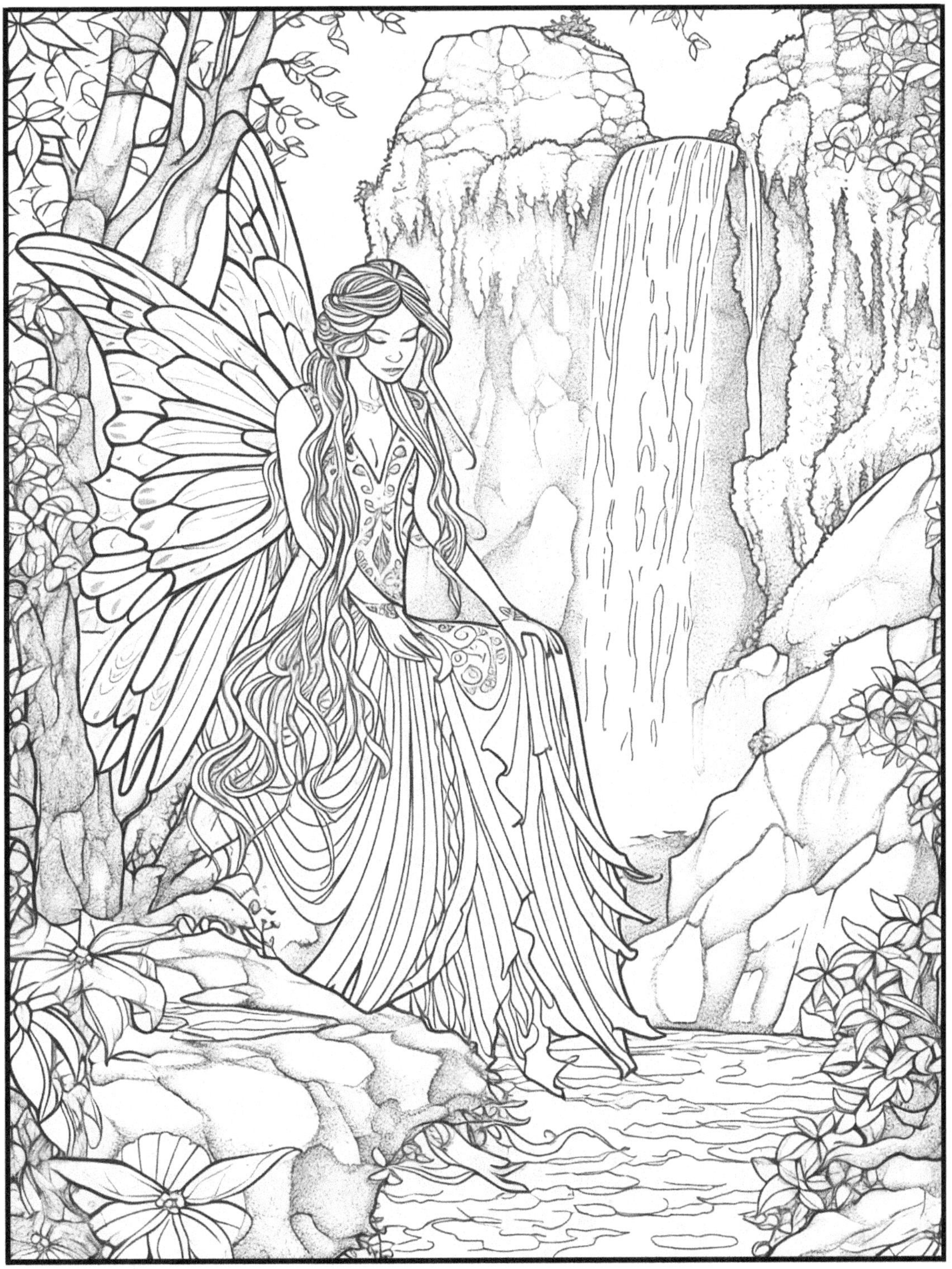

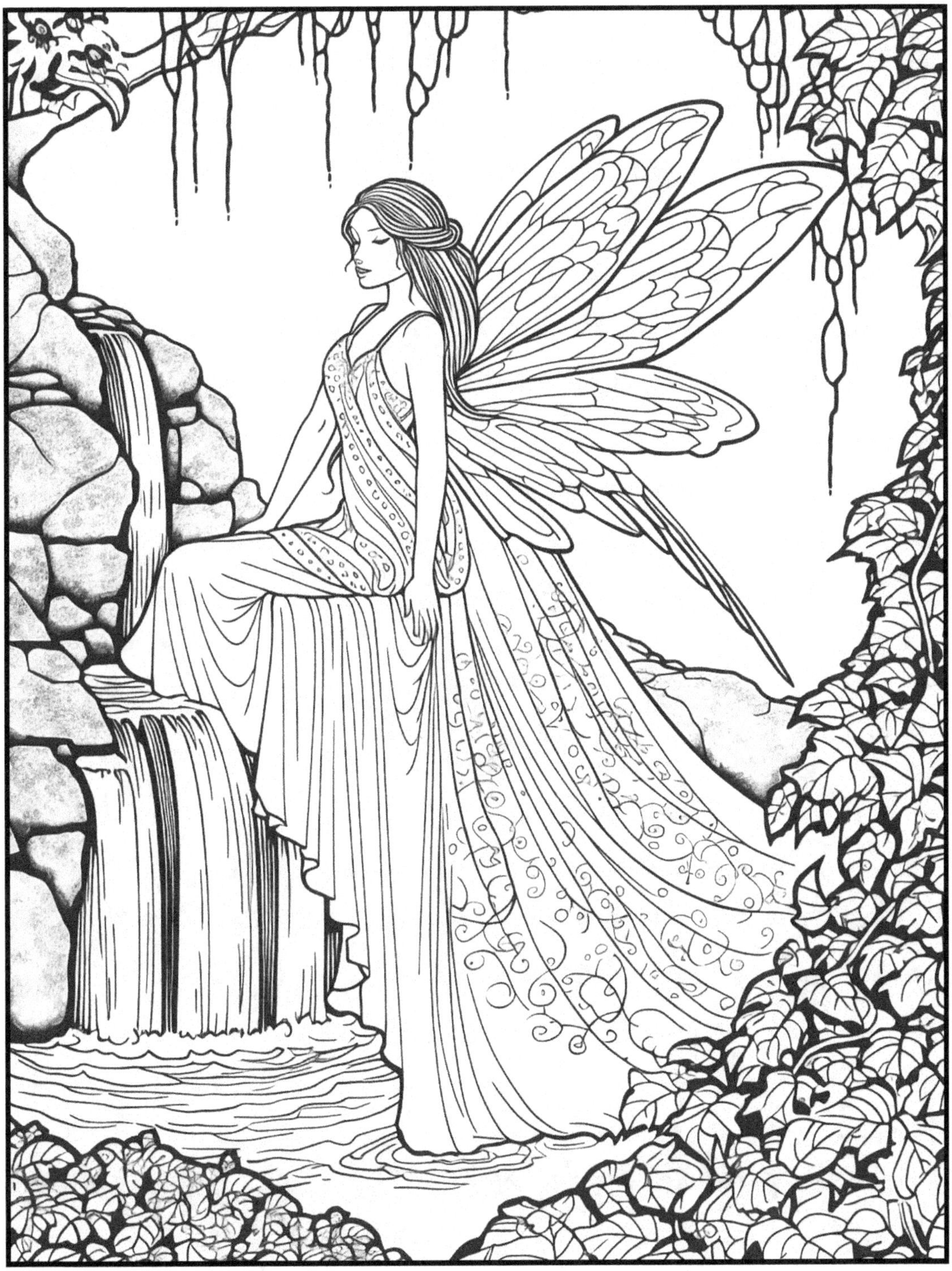

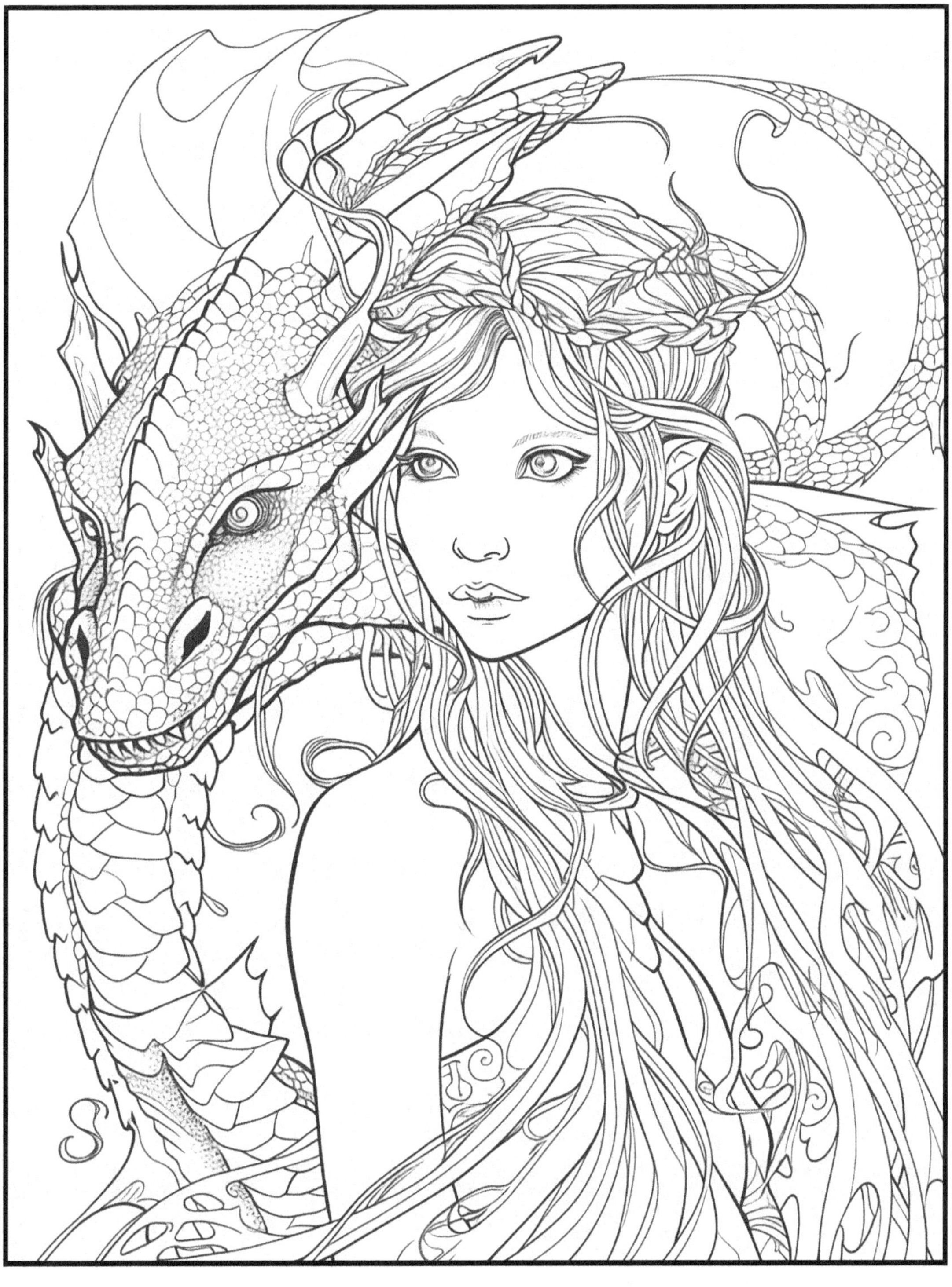

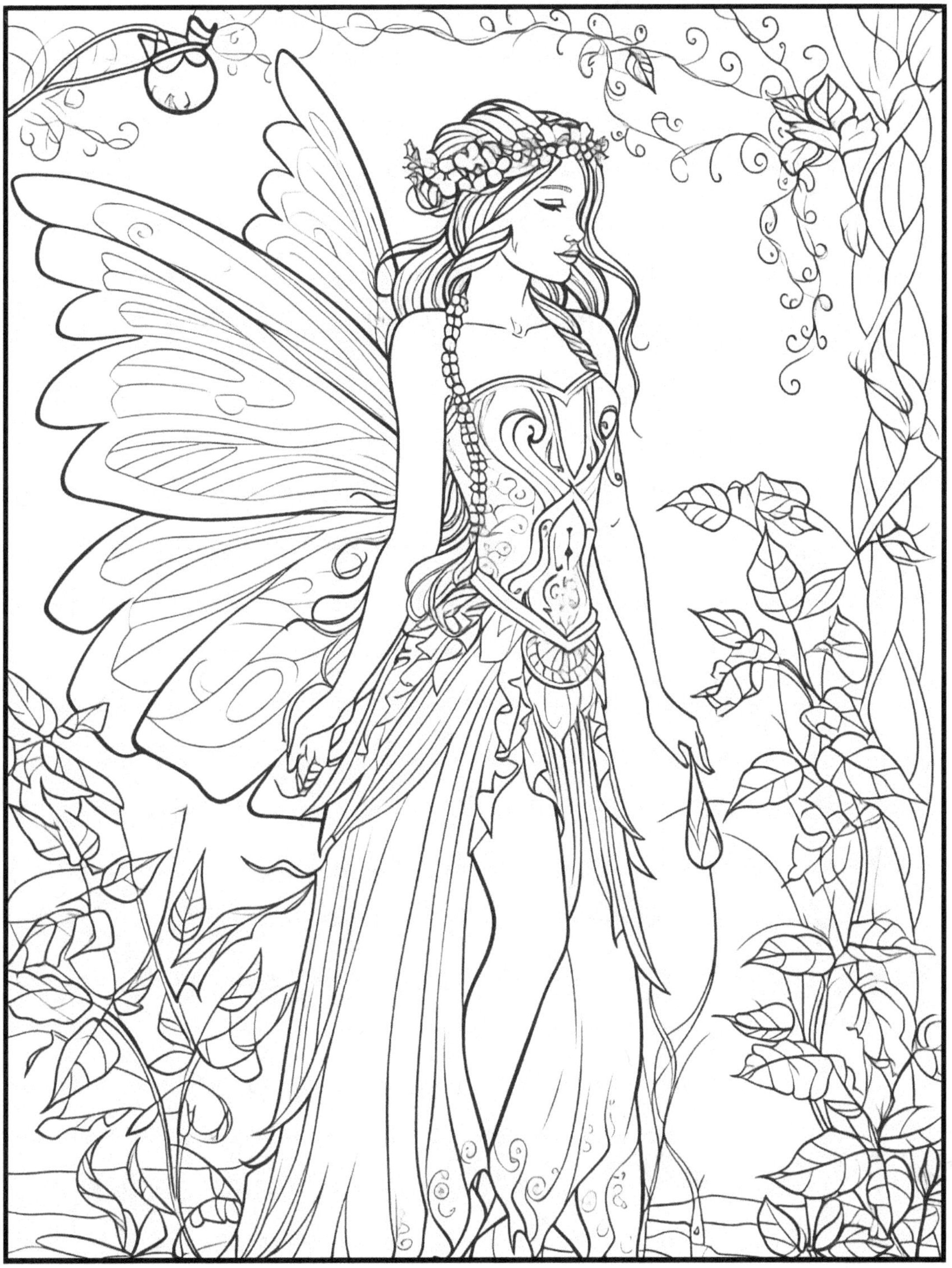

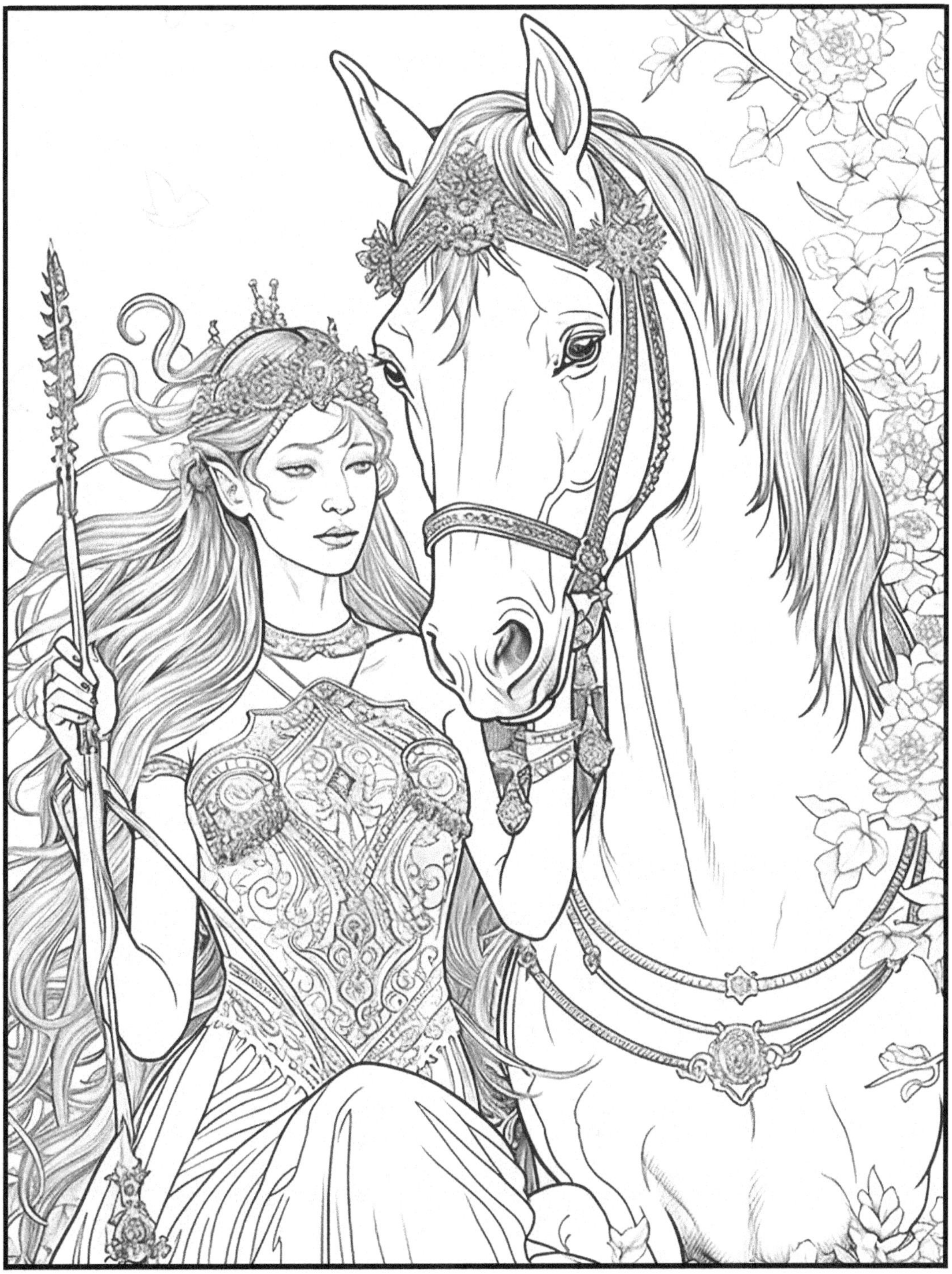

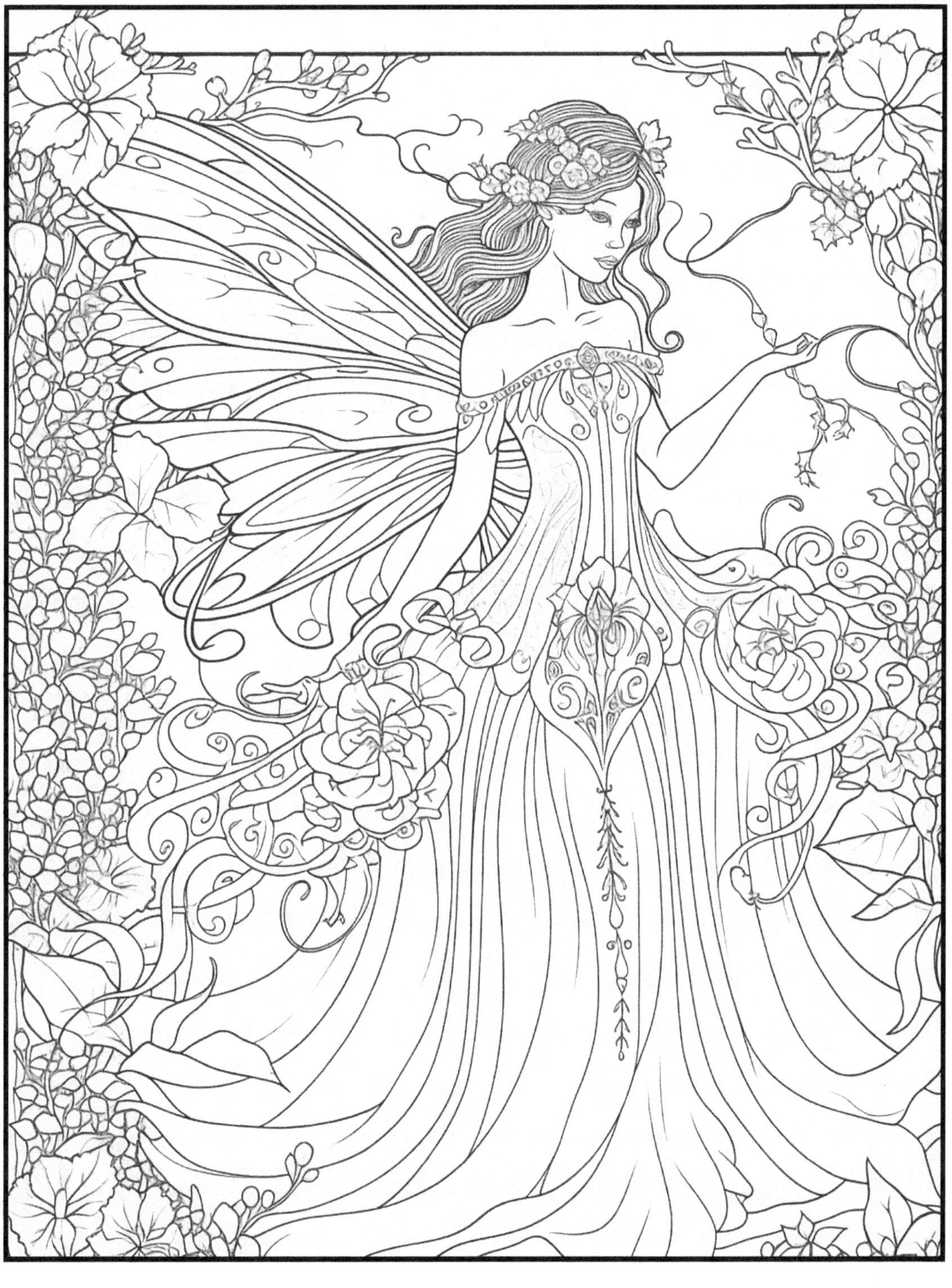

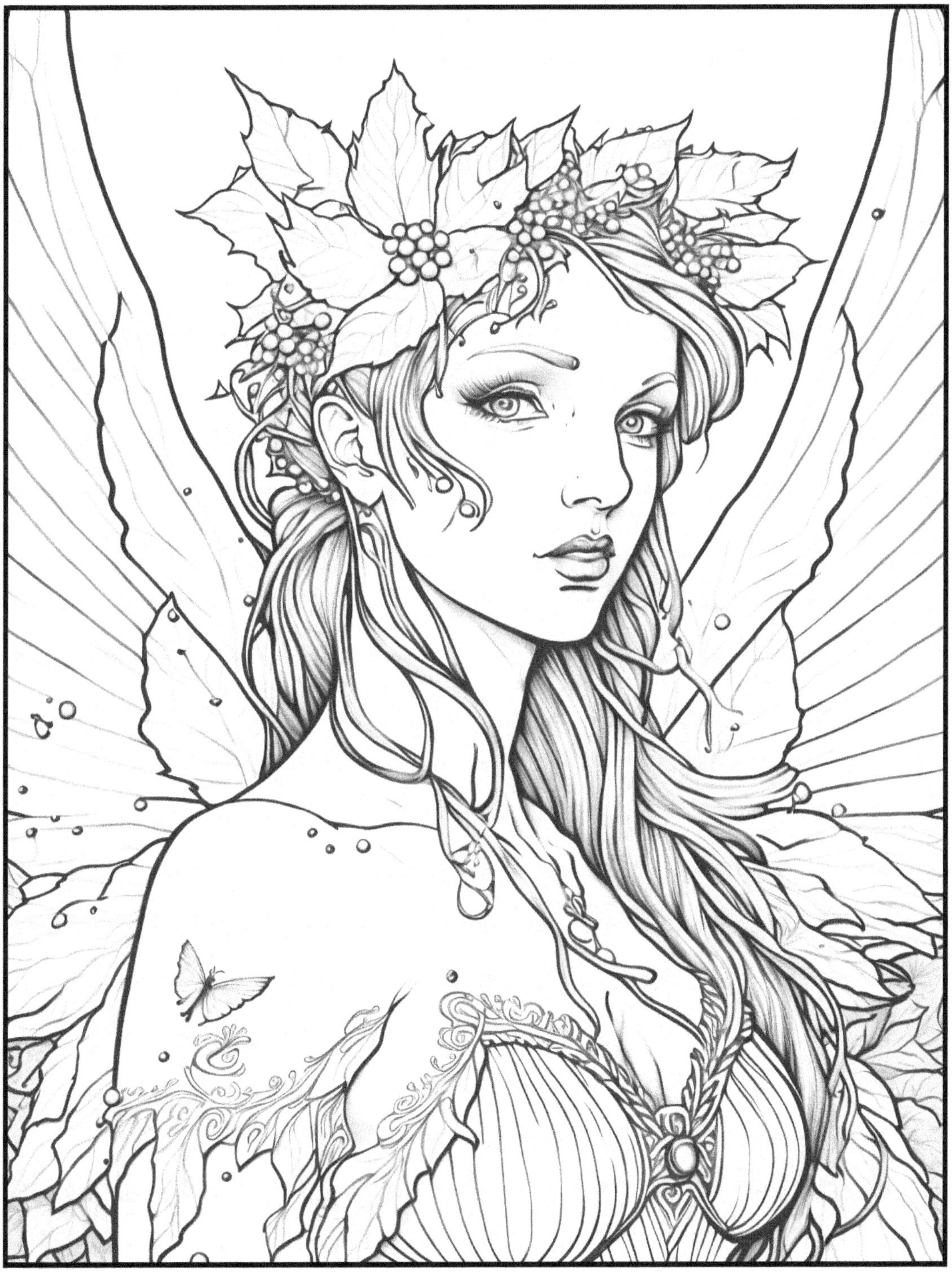

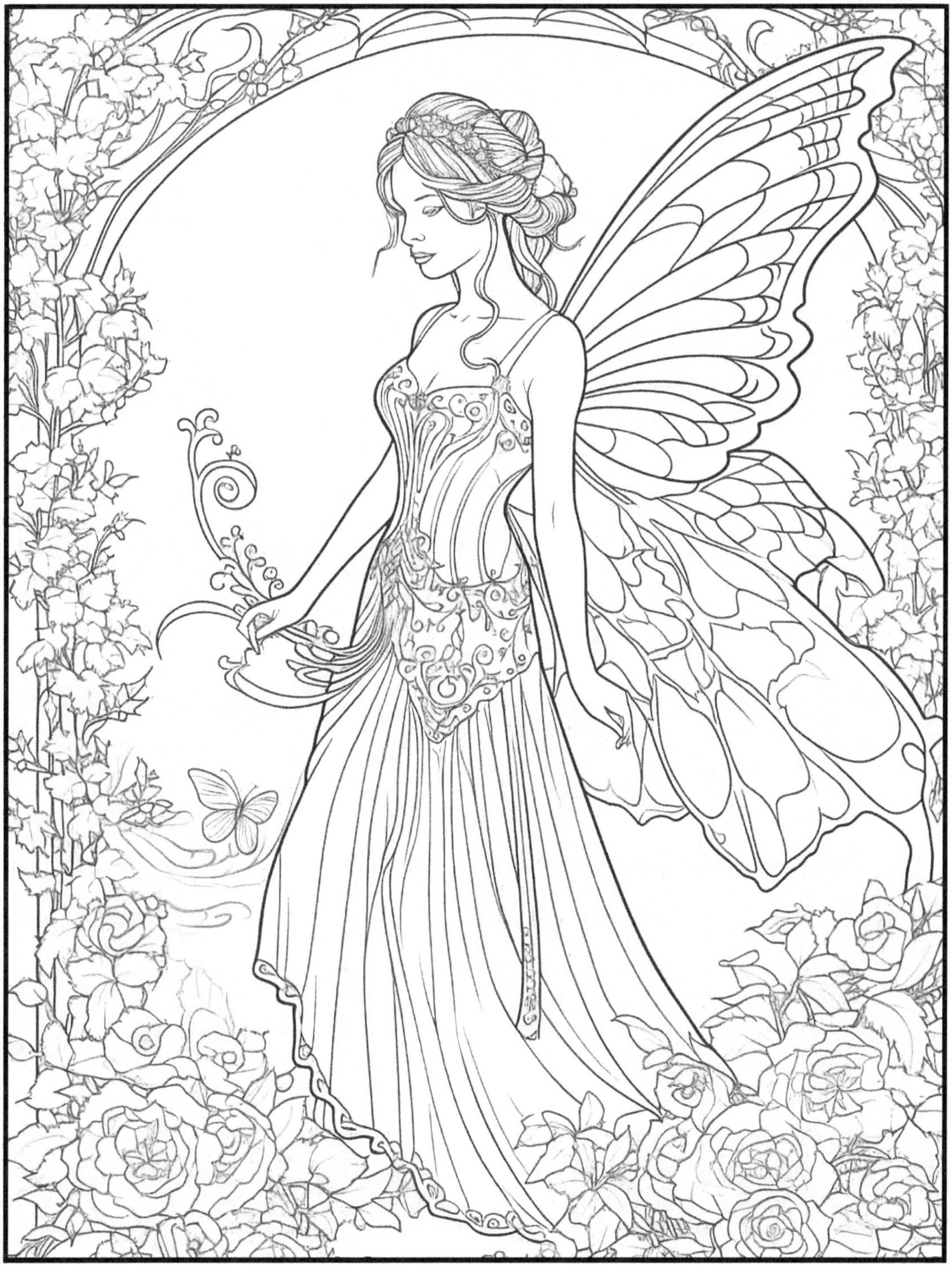

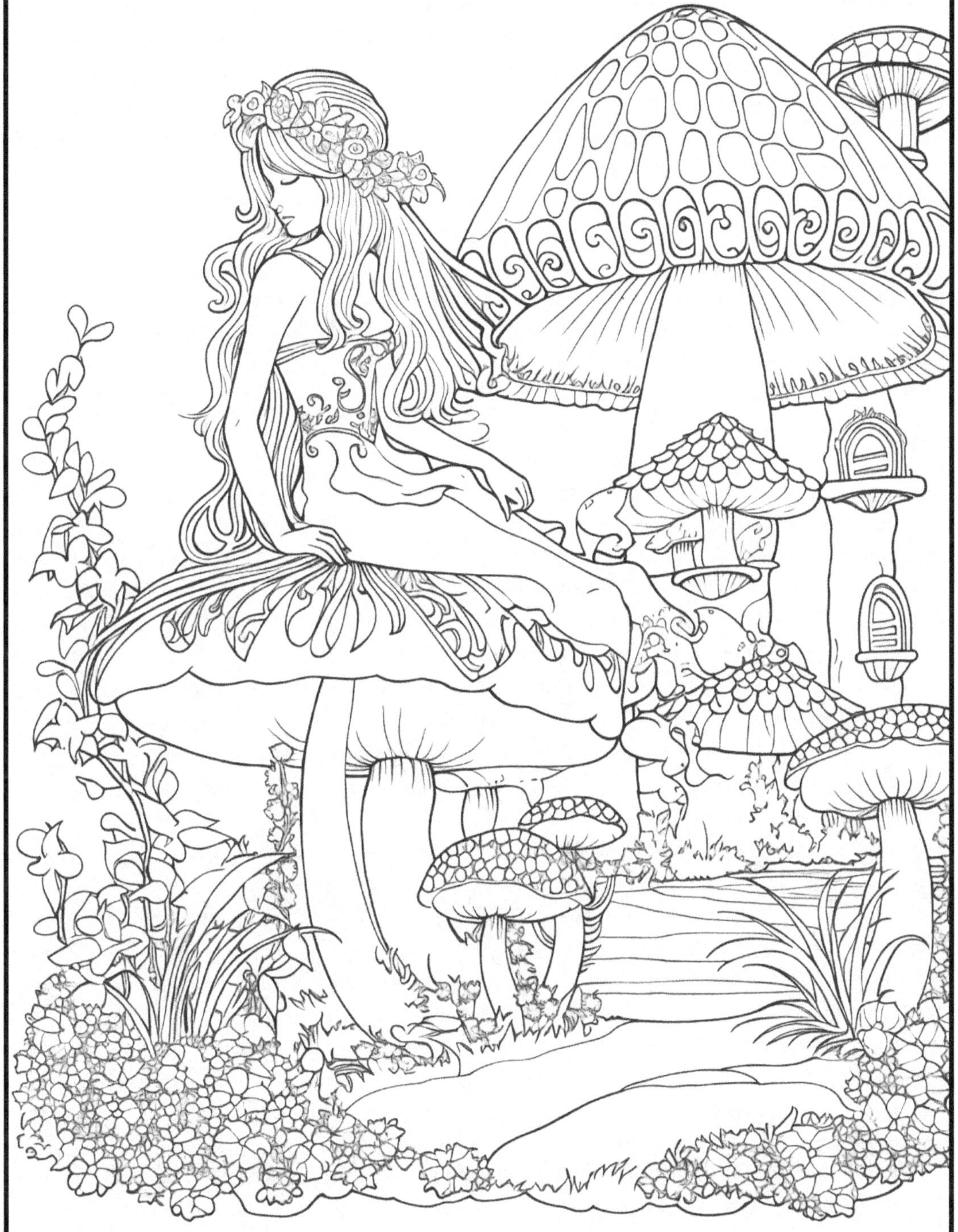

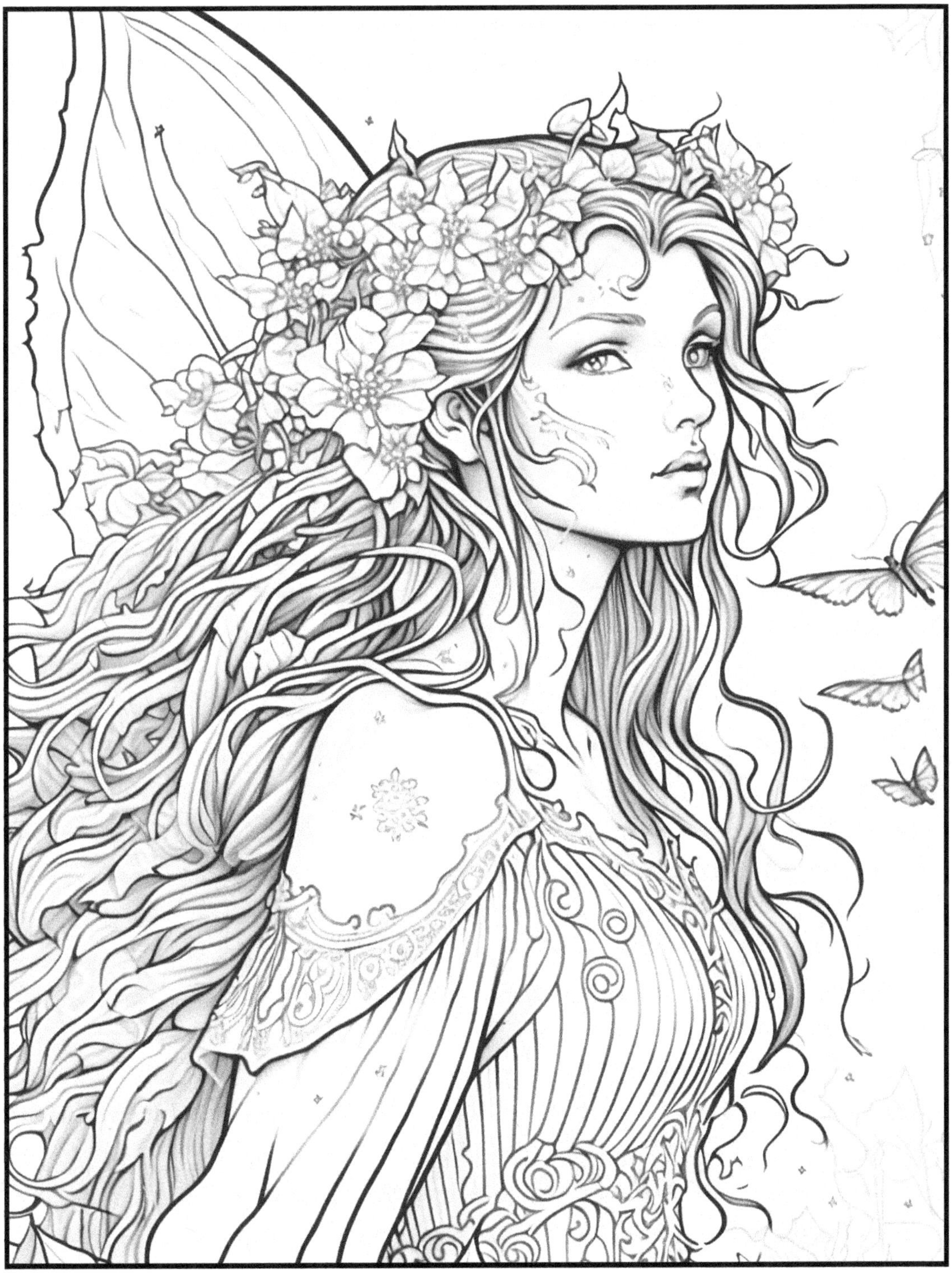

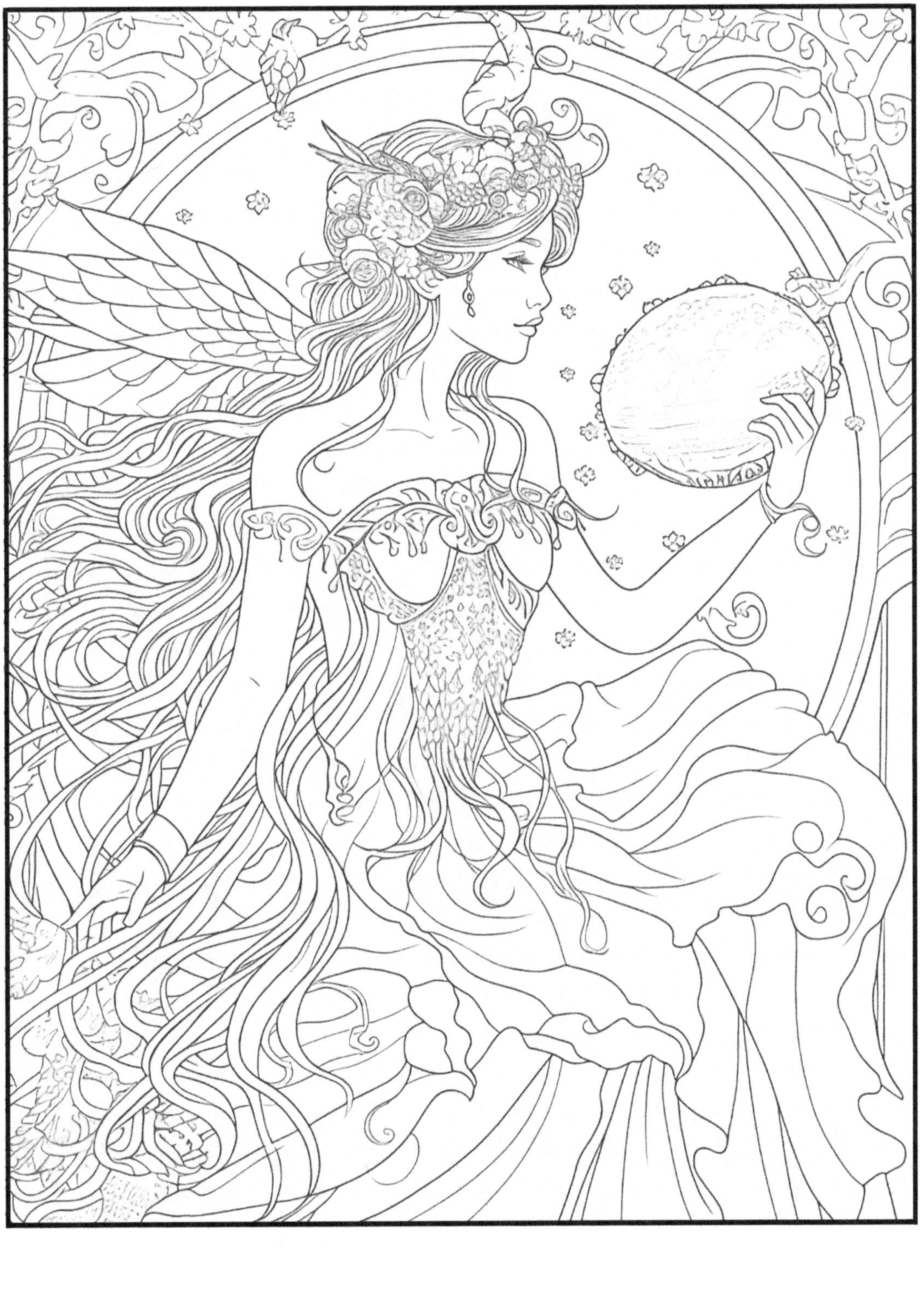

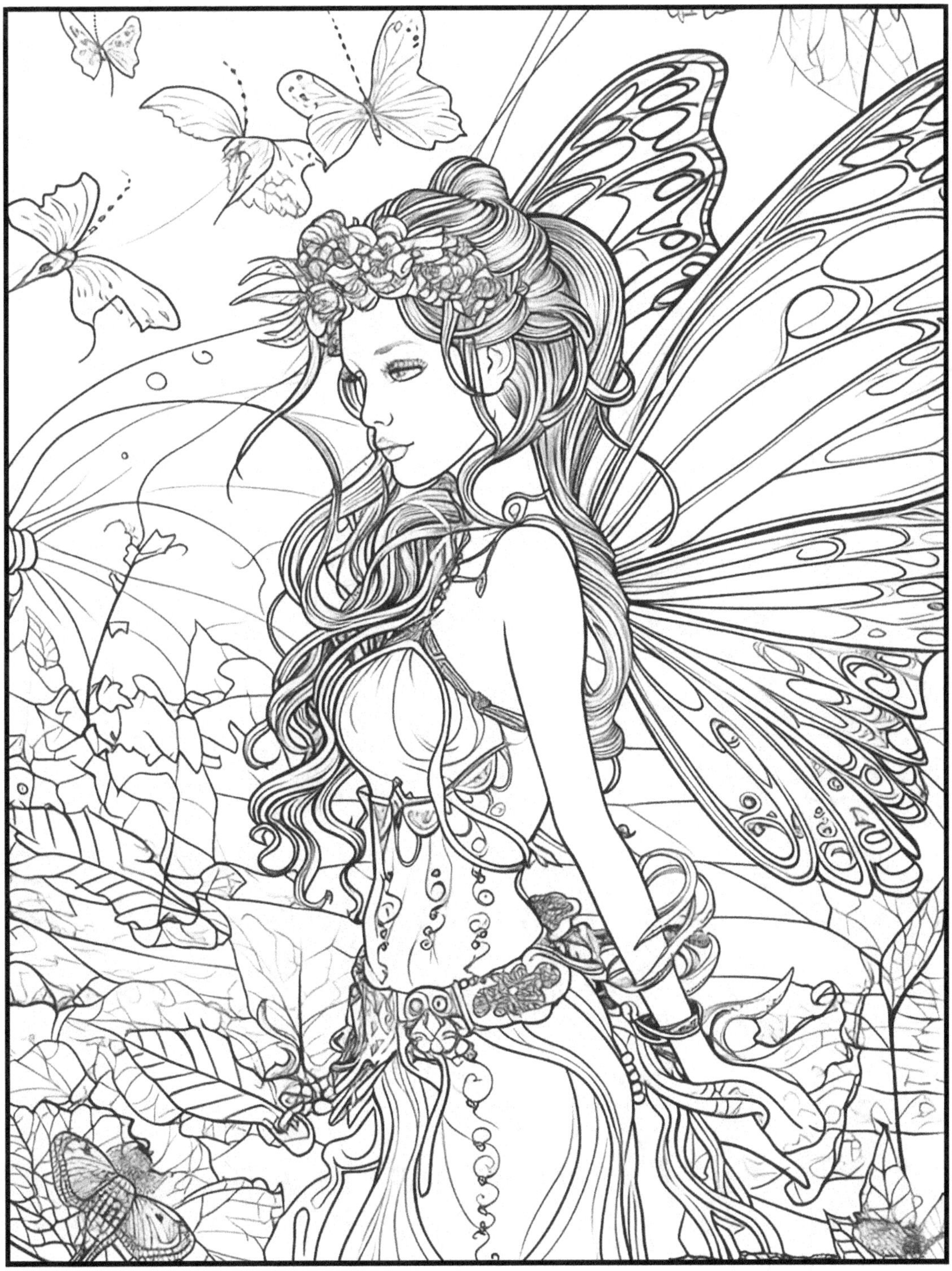

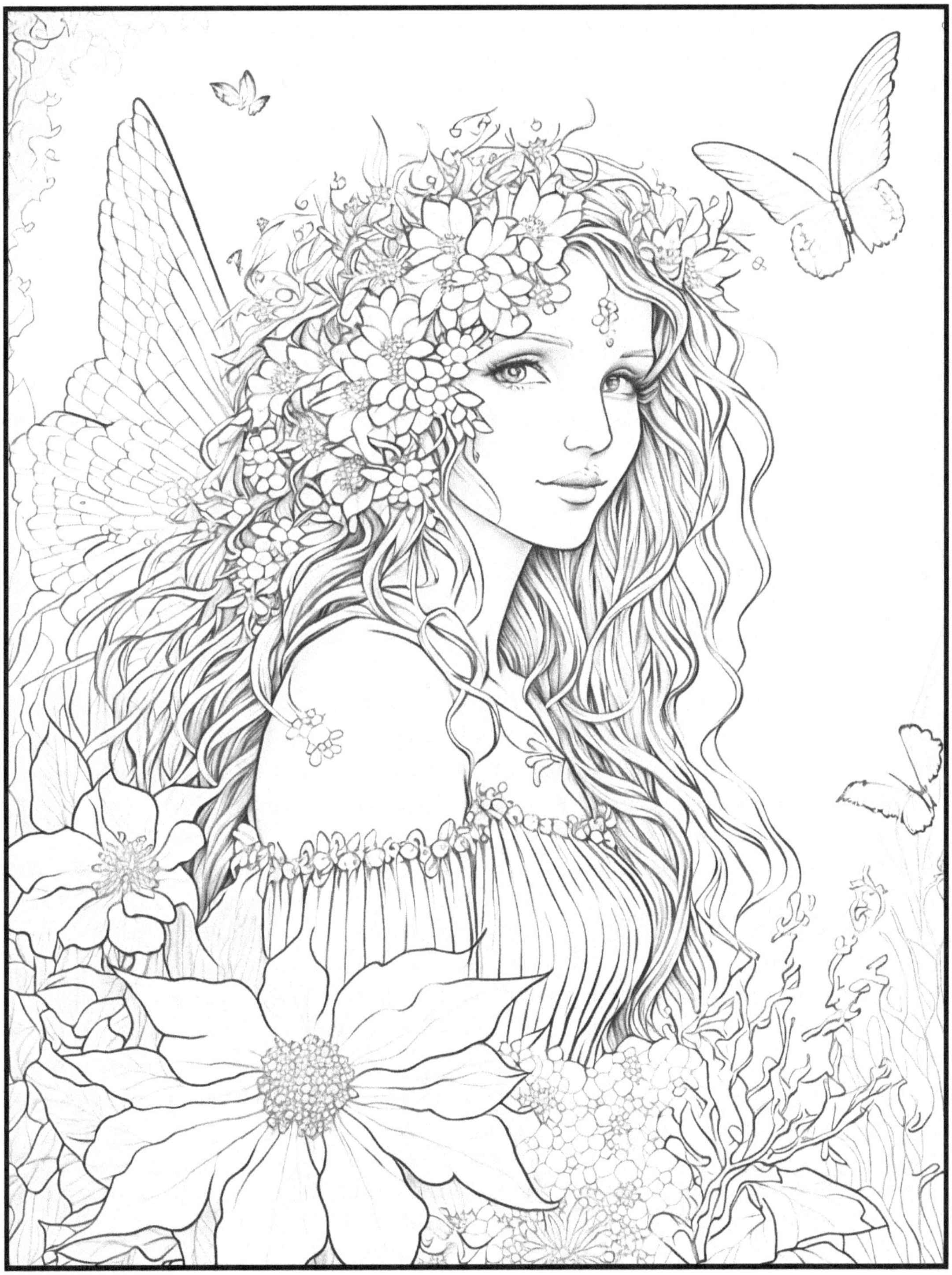

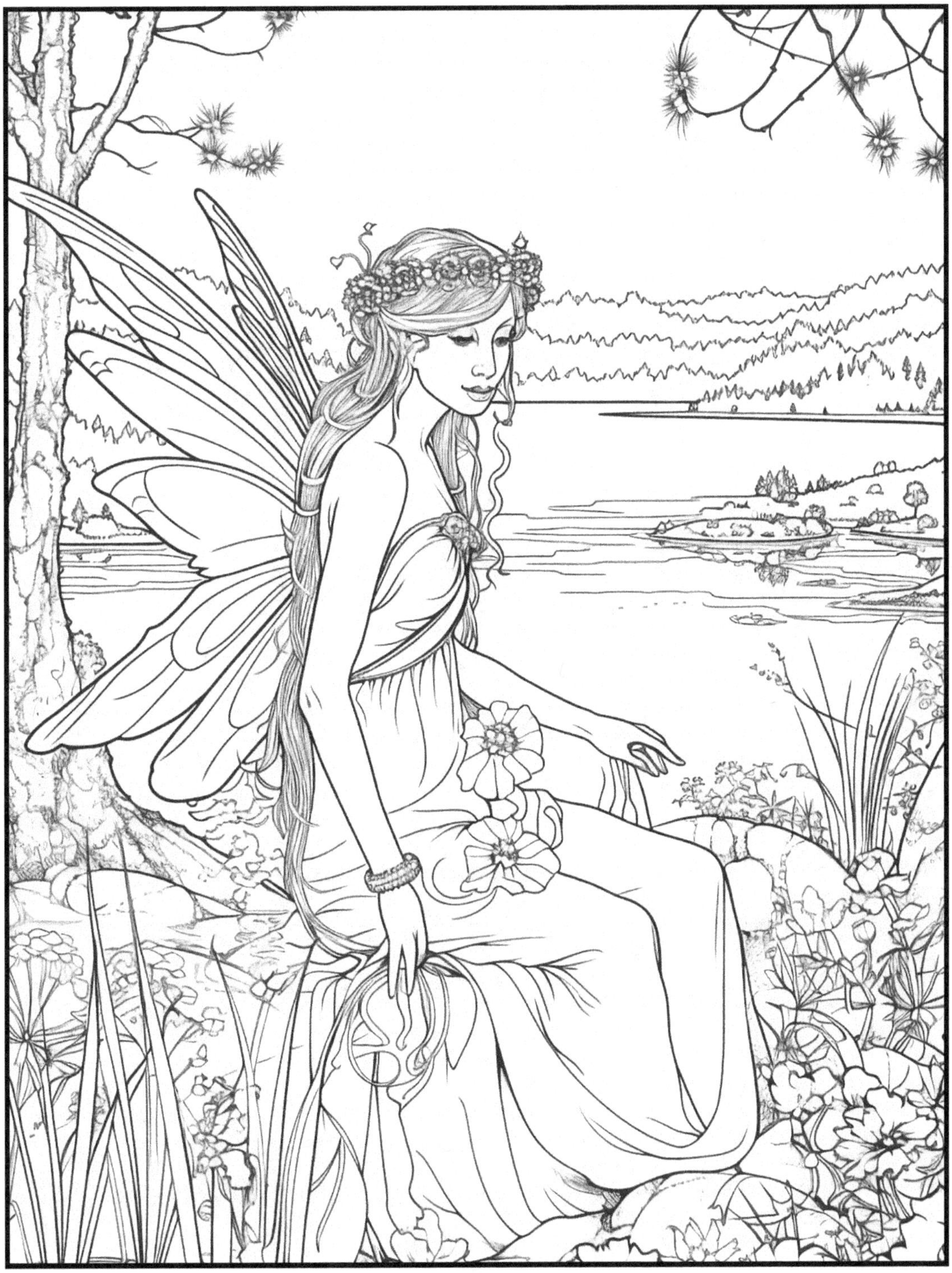

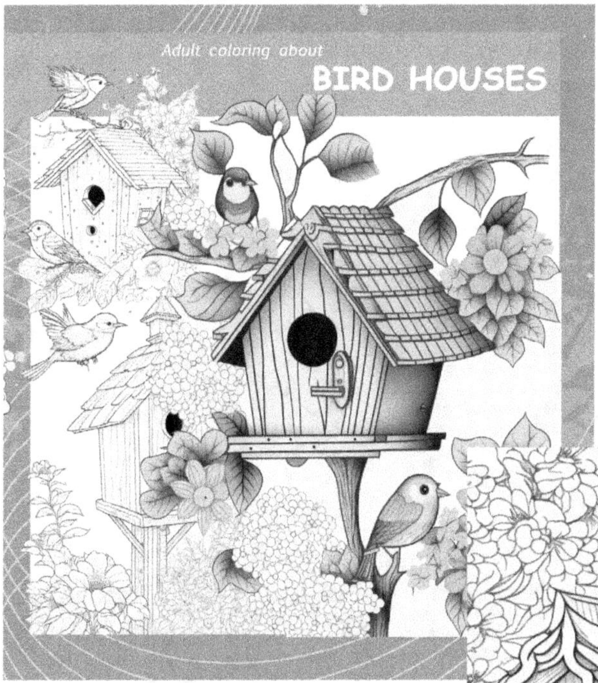

Also available

Adult coloring book

About Bird houses

Anna Apple

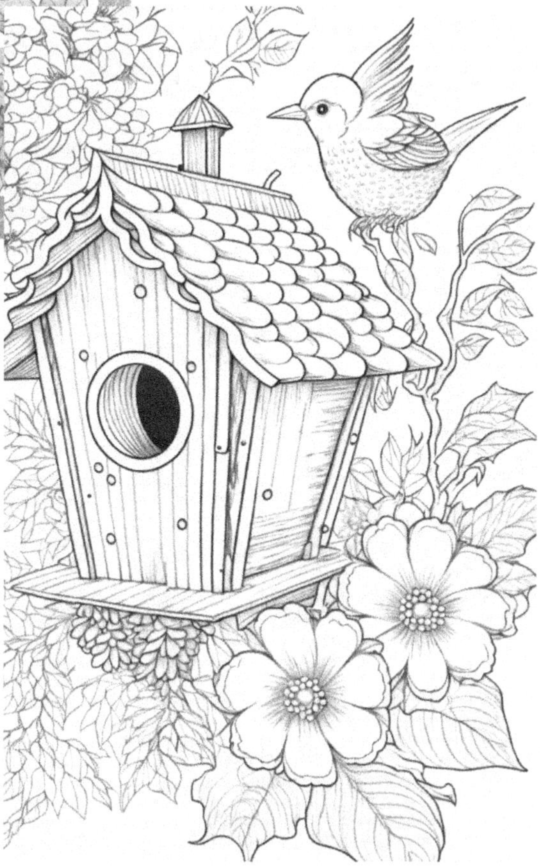

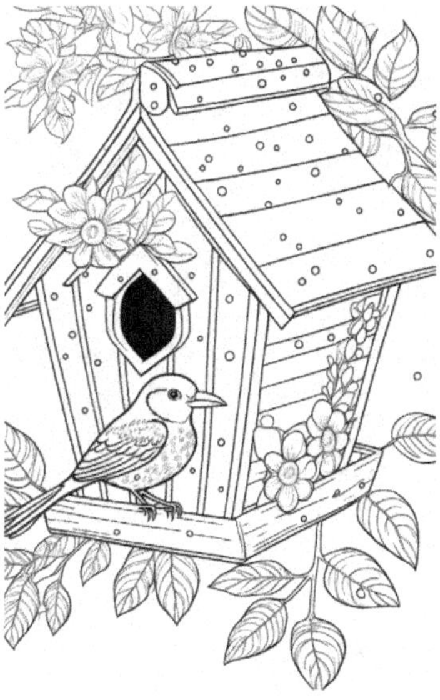

More books available
Online or local bookstores

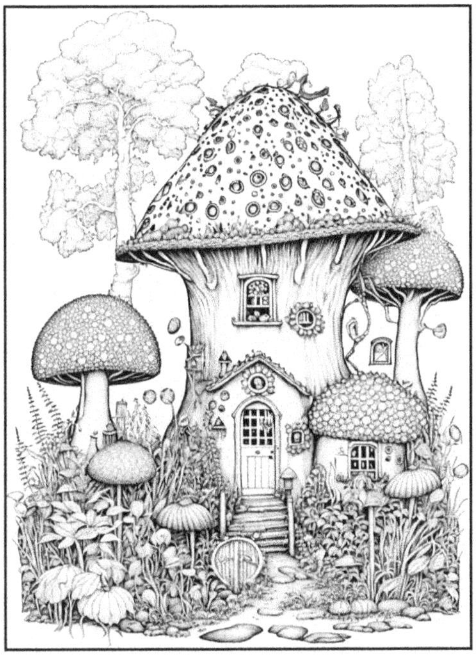

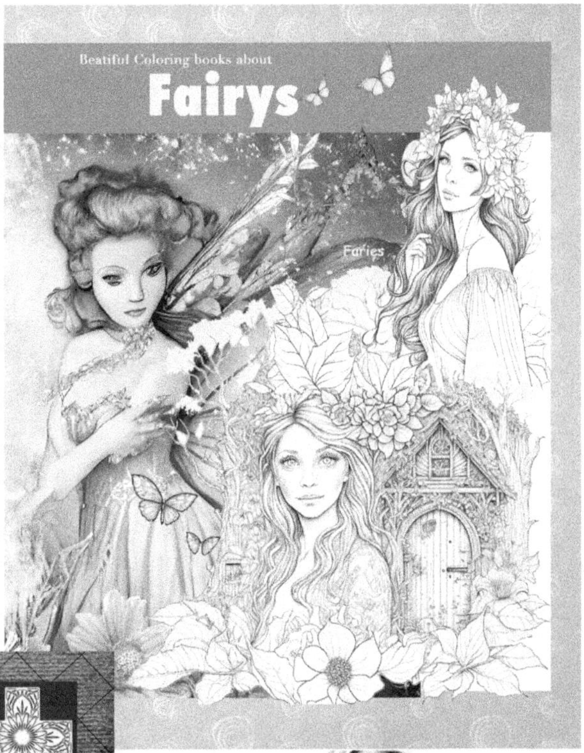

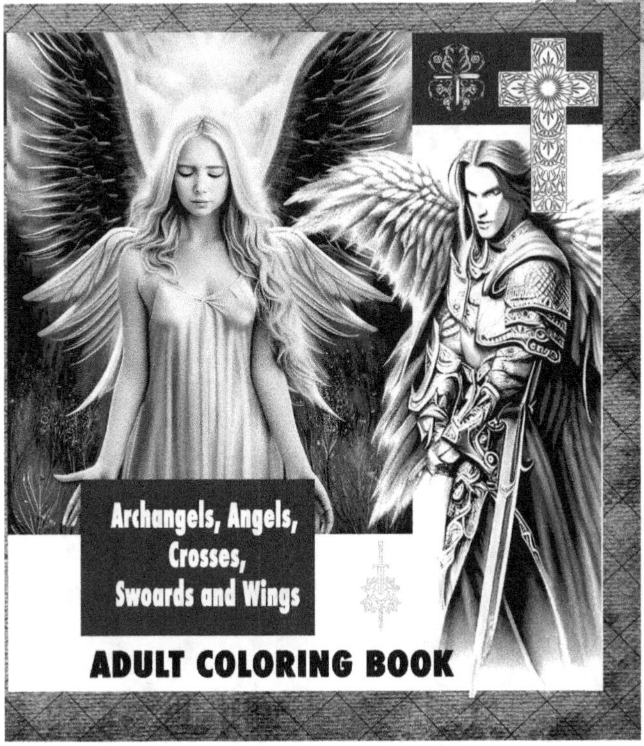

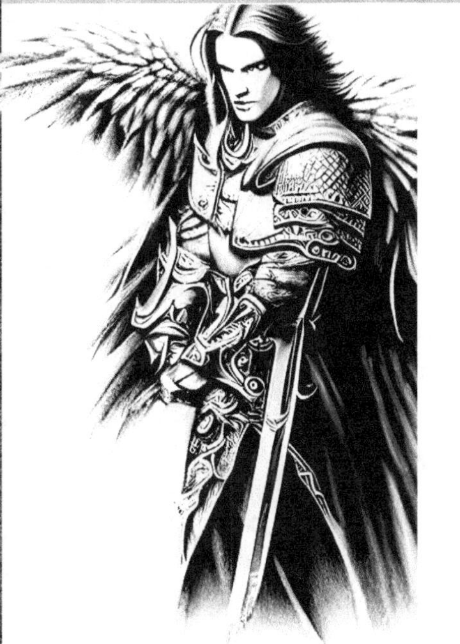

Thank you for your purchase.

Please leave a review, I would appreciate your feedback.

Anna Apple

www.ingramcontent.com/pod-product-compliance
Lightning Source LLC
Chambersburg PA
CBHW080901220526
45467CB00008B/2584
9798392670499